BOOK OF PRAYERS

... A PRAYER GUIDE TO HELP YOU CRY OUT TO
GOD IN EVERY SEASON!

JAMES TAIWO

PREFACE

Prayer, throughout ages, has been an essential tool to unlock the door of blessings for people that believe in God. Prayer rewards those who engage in it, however the task itself is often considered difficult to achieve. Satan always tries to halt people's mood for prayer when God has intended to bless them with it.

As a Christian and a normal human being, I have had my moments when I felt I did not know how to express myself in prayer. Weight of needs rolled in, and pressure of life culminated into making it a rigorous effort. In a quest for confronting life situations and over-coming them, I have sought for prayer guides, samples, and Bible references that can lead me into the presence of God.

Love is sharing! While God has helped me many times through prayers to overcome my challenges, he would not expect me to keep the discoveries to myself - without sharing. Under God's divine guid-ance, I prepared and collated this Book of Prayers for your benefits.

This handy book that covers a variety of prayer samples with applic-able Bible references will forever change your life for excellence!

As the Scripture charged *"Pray without season,"* I also admonish that you pray these Holy Spirit inspired prayers with an expectation to receive God's blessings. At the same time, I pray that may God of heaven in his infinite mercy grant your heart desires, and make your face shine with testimony – For in the name of Jesus Christ I have prayed. Amen!

To God Almighty who owns all the glory

PRAYER OF AUTHORITY

Our Lord Jesus Christ has authority over whatever situation we are passing through – Even the storms obey him! The Bible recorded:

"And the same day, when the evening has come, was come, he saith unto them; Let us pass over unto the other side. And when they had sent away the multitude, they took him even as he was on the ship. And there were also with him other little ships.

And there arose a great storm of wind, and the waves beat into the ship so that it was now full. And he was in the hinder part of the ship, asleep on a pillow: and they awake him, and say unto him, Master, carest thou not that we perish? And he arose, and rebuked the wind, and said unto the sea, Peace, be still. And the wind ceased, and there was a great calm. And he said unto them, Why are ye so fearful? How is it that ye have no faith? And they feared exceedingly, and said one to another, what manner of man is this, that even the wind and the sea obey him?" (Mark 4:35-41 KJV)

---

* * *

Exercise your Authority through Prayers

1

I believe in the power of God to overcome whatever problem may come my way. In the name of Jesus Christ, I command all works of Satan in my life to fail. I remove every root of sickness, pain, and sorrow. By the authority in the name of Jesus Christ I command every negative situation to turn positive. From now on, I will enjoy the deliverance of God, and my testimony shall abide. For in the name of Jesus Christ I have exercised my authority. Amen.

2

I am a child of God and his Holy Spirit dwells in me to have victory in every situation. Therefore, I command in the name of Jesus Christ that every stronghold of the enemy against me must be destroyed! I rebuke Satan and bind his evil forces; I cast them out of my life. By the authority of Jesus Christ, I remove every root of sickness, poverty, failure, and any other negative activity from my life. I replace all evil with goodness. I convert sickness to good health, poverty to riches, and failure to success. My testimony of victory shall remain and abide from now on and forever more! For in the name of Jesus Christ I decree! Amen.

3

By the authority in the name of Jesus Christ, I receive forgiveness of sins. Trials and temptations of the enemy can no more overpower me since I have reserved my faith in Jesus Christ. From now on, I receive the power of the Holy Spirit to live an acceptance life before God. I receive God's strength to live triumphantly every day of my life. I shall prevail in every situation of life, and by God's grace I shall inherit eternal life in heaven. My declaration of faith is made through faith in Jesus Christ my Lord. Amen!

PRAYER OF MIRACLE

A miracle is an event not explicable by natural or scientific law, which must only be attributed to God. One of such events was recorded in the Bible when Jesus Christ turned water into wine after all hope was lost during a wedding at the Canaan of Galilee.

"Now there were six stone water jars there for the Jewish rites of purification, each holding twenty or thirty gallons. Jesus said to the servants, "Fill the jars with water." And they filled them up to the brim. And he said to them, "Now draw some out and take it to the master of the feast." So, they took it. When the master of the feast tasted the water now become wine, and did not know where it came from (though the servants who had drawn the water knew), the master of the feast called the bridegroom and said to him," Everyone serves the good wine first, and when people have drunk freely, then the poor wine. But you have kept the good wine until now." This, the first of his signs, Jesus did at Cana in Galilee and

manifested his glory. And his disciples believed in him." (John 2:1-11 ESV)

---

* * *

Pray the Prayer of Miracle

1

Heavenly Lord, I believe you are God of miracle, and you will surely perform your miracles to my advantage! Therefore, I am asking that you stand on my behalf to show yourself strong and glorify your name. Please silence my enemies and override their evil desires against my life. Fight my battles and give me victory! Let me have rest in every aspect of my life so that I can have a testimony and glorify your holy name. For in the name of Jesus Christ I pray. Amen.

2

Almighty God, I know you have enough power to handle difficult situations. I know you can help me; therefore, I am asking that you give me the grace to call on you during crisis. Teach me how to pray and help me to demonstrate faith! Let every meditation of my heart receive your favorable answer, and let me live long to enjoy your benefits in the land of the living. For in the name of Jesus Christ I pray. Amen.

3

Everlasting Father, please empower me to pray always. Help me to use prayers to conquer my life battles. Let me use prayers to address and overcome all circumstances that challenge my faith, peace, and progress. Please grant all my heart desires when I call and let it be well with me throughout the days of my life. For in the name of Jesus Christ I pray. Amen.

PRAYER OF SUPPLICATION

Supplication literally means "a request or petition". In spiritual context, a person who makes supplication humbly presents his requests before God – With an expectation that He will answer them. Daniel, in the Bible, was prohibited by King Darius to offer prayer to any deity than himself. Daniel defied the king's rule and made his supplication to the living God.

Christians are to daily offer their supplications to God in form of thanksgiving and making petition for their needs. The Bible says:

"Be anxious for nothing, but in everything by prayer and supplication, with thanksgiving, let your requests be made known to God." (Philippians 4:6 NIV)

* * *

Pray the Prayer of Supplication

1

Eternal Rock of Ages, I ask in the name of your Son Jesus Christ to please bless, heal, restore, and promote me. Please let all my requests be granted, and let my mouth be filled with laughter. For in the name of Jesus Christ I pray. Amen.

2

Heavenly Lord, please make me your good steward who satisfies your heart desires at all time. Do not let me sin. Also, help me to repent of my sins whenever I wrong you. Let me maintain a good relationship with you, and let me enjoy your benefits throughout the days of my life. For in the name of Jesus Christ I pray. Amen.

3

Father, please do not let your wonders cease in my life. Let me obtain your grace so that I can be selected for special assignments that would glorify your name throughout the world. Once I am anointed, please keep me humble so that I can be used immensely, and so that your name can be glorified more than ever before. For in the name of Jesus Christ I pray. Amen.

4

Oh my God, I want to be rich, but I do not want to go to hell fire! Help me to pursue clean riches, and let me honor you with my resources. Let me utilize my riches to serve you and meet other people's needs. Do not let me be punished, but let me be duly rewarded on earth and in heaven also. For in the name of Jesus Christ I pray. Amen.

5

Dear God, please help me to place my absolute trust in you. Help me to love and trust people, but let my absolute trust be placed in you. Let me trust, pray, and look up to you for all my needs. I understand and believe that you will send me the necessary people to meet my needs at all times. Let my absolute trust be reserved in you at all times, so that I can live successfully and happily on earth. For in the name of Jesus Christ I pray. Amen.

6

Oh Lord, please do not let me provoke you with sin so that I will not incur your terrible judgment. Do not let me abuse your grace, but help me to duly follow all your instructions so that it can be well with me on earth. Also, please help me to repent of my sins whenever I realize that I have sinned against you. For in the name of Jesus Christ I pray. Amen.

7

Oh Lord, I prefer to receive little blessings that to receive huge curses. Therefore, I am determined to honor you and respect your servants so that I can prosper. Please do not let me take you or your servants for granted, but help me to give due honor to whom it belongs so that I can prosper in the land of the living. For in the name of Jesus Christ I pray. Amen.

8

Father, let me be a good parent who will encourage my children to bring out their best virtues. Help me to be sensitive to recognize the traits that will benefit them. Once I am aware of their traits, give me the grace to properly direct them, so that they can be successful. I also pray the same prayer for all parents and those who aspire to be parents. For in the name of Jesus Christ I pray. Amen.

9

Dear Jesus, please empower me to preach the gospel at all time - whether convenient or not. Help me to understand the need for evangelism, and help me to evangelize gospel to your satisfaction. Anoint me with grace to explain the gospel in a way that will yield positive rewards for your kingdom. As I share the gospel, let unbelievers submit their faith to Jesus Christ and be saved. In addition, please bless me, and let me receive your due reward for obeying your instructions. For in the name of Jesus Christ I pray. Amen.

10

Father, I look up to you for help during my time of needs. I invite you into my situations, and I beg you to help me. Please provide solutions to all my problems, and let your goodness manifest in my life to the fullness. Also, confuse my enemies and let them stumble at their evil plots and imaginations. For in the name of Jesus Christ I pray. Amen.

11

Eternal Rock of Ages, I understand that you are the king of the universe; you have all things at disposal, and nothing is difficult for you to do. Therefore, I invite your presence into my situations, and I ask for your help. Please, subdue every mountain of challenges that surround me. Level all mountains of sickness, poverty, and all forms of attacks. Award me victory and give me laughter. Let me rejoice and celebrate your goodness in the land of the living. For in the name of Jesus Christ I pray. Amen.

PRAYER OF DILIGENCE

Christians ought to be dedicated in their spiritual journey in order to meet God in heaven. Also, believers must be committed to their earthly tasks so as to prosper on earth. Diligence is one of God's laid down principles as recorded in the scripture:

"And let us not grow weary of doing good, for in due season we will reap if we do no give up" (Galatians 6:9 ESV)

---

* * *

Pray the Prayer of Diligence

1

Father, please help me to patiently wait for your promises to be fulfilled in my life. Do not let me be over ambitious, but help me to work within your plans. Also, enable me to be hardworking and meticulous, so that I can have astounding success. Let me be satisfied with your blessings, and let me remain grateful to you throughout the days of my life. For in the name of Jesus Christ I pray. Amen.

2

Jehovah, I understand that it is necessary that I trust you so that I can see your promises fulfilled over my life. Therefore, I ask that you please give me the grace to keep serving you diligently. Let my confidence in you be resolute; let me cooperate with you so that I can have all my expectations met. Please give me long life, good health, and prosperity to continue enjoying your goodness in the land of the living. For in the name of Jesus Christ I pray. Amen.

3

Dear Jesus Christ, please give me the grace to be a focus Christian who will faithfully serve you throughout the days of my life. Help me to wait, watch, and pray for your second coming. Keep me fit to be qualified for the rapture, and let me receive your imperishable crown of glory in heaven. I also pray that you please save the unbelievers so that they too can be qualified to enter into your eternal kingdom. For in the name of Jesus Christ I make my requests. Amen.

PRAYER FOR THE GIFT OF WISDOM

Wisdom is one of the gifts of the Holy Spirit that God uses to help Christians do the unimaginable. The gift of wisdom helps a person to make decisions from God's perspectives. Such person will simultaneously grow in God's fear and make decisions that will benefit his life. The gift of wisdom is not earned earthly by experience or education; it comes by relying on the Holy Spirit.

"If any of you lacks wisdom, let him ask of God, who gives to all liberally and without reproach, and it will be given to him." (James 1:5 NKJV)

Pray for the Gift of Wisdom

1

Oh Lord, you are the father of wisdom, and I want you to shower me with wisdom. Let me have self-control. Give me the grace to accurately process my thoughts, and guide my actions to reflect wisdom. Let my wisdom be selfless, so that it can last long and also lead me to heaven. For in the name of Jesus Christ I pray. Amen.

2

Dear God, I desire your wisdom more than silver and gold. I want to be wise so that I can always make appropriate decisions that will benefit your kingdom and me. I understand that I may not receive your wisdom unless I commit myself to the consistent studying of the scriptures. Therefore, I ask you to please help me to be disciplined and consistently study the bible. Let me observe all your instructions so that I can be wise, and so that I can prosper in life. For in the name of Jesus Christ I pray. Amen.

3

Father, please make me a wise person! I understand that wisdom makes a difference between success and failure. I also realized that no one can have an abiding success without godly wisdom that comes through conscious godly fear; therefore, let me fear you. Bless me with incorruptible wisdom that will earn me an abiding success. Let my blessings stand out so that all people may praise your name on my behalf. For in the name of Jesus Christ I pray. Amen.

PRAYER OF POWER TO DO EXPLOITS

The almighty God is always looking for believers through whom He can display His extraordinary power. He wants to demonstrate his remarkable ability that will showcase his greatness through us.

"And such as do wickedly against the covenant shall he corrupt by flatteries: but the people that do know their God shall be strong, and do exploits." (Daniel 11:32 KJV)

---

* * *

Pray for Power to do Exploits

1

Dear Lord Jesus Christ, I understand that you have supernatural power to heal and save people. Some people have experienced your power, and I want to share the same experience also. I believe that I will be endowed with power to perform signs and wonders once I confess my faith in you. Therefore, I declare my relentless faith in you today that you are the Son of God, and you are the savior. Henceforth, energize me with your divine anointing to start performing wonders and exploits. For in your precious Name I Pray. Amen.

2

In the name of Jesus Christ, I receive the power of God to preach the irresistible gospel. I also claim the strength and grace of God to preach the gospel that will lead sinners to repentance and have access to the kingdom of God. Let the Holy Spirit come upon me, and let him empower me to do exploits for his kingdom. For in the name of Jesus Christ I make my declarations. Amen.

3

Dear God, I believe your scripture that states, "I can do all things through Christ who strengthens me" (Philippians 4:13). Therefore, I ask you to please empower me through the Holy Spirit to do exploits. Let me succeed in all my endeavors, so that I can share your testimony of goodness to other people. For in the name of Jesus Christ I make my requests. Amen.

PRAYER OF BLESSING

The word "blessing" was mentioned more than seven thousand times in the bible. This shows how important it is to God and believers. God would bless his children in many ways; we must be thankful once we have received his goodness. The scripture says:

> *"The LORD bless thee, and keep thee: The LORD make his face shine upon thee, and be gracious unto thee: The LORD lift up his countenance upon thee and give thee peace."* (Numbers 6:24-26 KJV)

* * *

Pray the Prayer of Blessing

1

Father, please declare your promises of goodness on my life. I know that your promises are sure, and they will come to pass. Therefore, I ask that you please declare into my life good health, long life, and prosperity. Please help me to enjoy all your goodness from now and always. For in the name of Jesus Christ I pray. Amen.

2

Dear God, I understand that you usually bless people and make them rich by your grace; I want to enjoy the same benefits from you also. Therefore, I am determined to be your faithful child. I confess my faith in your Son Jesus Christ, and I accept him as my personal Lord and Savior. From now on, I will faithfully serve you; I pray that you please keep me fit to enjoy your benefits always. For in the name of Jesus Christ your Son – I pray. Amen.

3

Jehovah, I can realize that you hate laziness, and you will not bless a lazy person. Therefore, I ask that you please make me a hardworking person. Help me to be diligent in my work so that you can bless me. Let the fruits of my labors abide, and let me enjoy your blessings throughout the days of my life. For in the name of Jesus Christ I pray. Amen.

4

Oh, dear Lord, please teach me how to love you with all my heart. Help me to be loyal to you. Let me serve you with all honesty so that I can merit your lasting blessings. Anoint me through your Holy Spirit to remain fit for your kingdom. For in the name of Jesus Christ I pray. Amen.

5

Eternal Rock of ages, nothing is better than your blessing in anyone's life; I want you to bless me! Please bless me; I want your blessing at all cost! I understand that you cannot bless anyone who operates against your counsel. You will only bless people who engage in positive adventures; therefore, I have set my mind to cooperate with you. I will walk in your way so that I can be blessed. All I ask is the empowerment of your Holy Spirit to do what is appropriate. Please let your Holy Spirit guide me to be a positive child, and let your glory shine through me always. For in the name of Jesus Christ I pray. Amen.

6

Good Lord, please direct my steps to honor you in holiness, so that I can be qualified to receive your blessings. Also, give me the grace to be humble and truthfully repent whenever I sin. Let all my missed opportunities be restored and let me receive new benefits also so that I can share the testimony of your goodness throughout the world. For in the name of Jesus Christ I pray. Amen.

7

O dear good Lord, I want huge blessings from you! Shower me with your plentiful benefits. I understand that someone may not receive a tangible blessing from you without committing to your gospel. Also, you may refuse to bless an inconsistent Christian. Therefore, I ask for your grace to be committed in my relationship with you. Help me to be active in Christian circle, and enable me with grace to support and participate in gospel evangelization so that your salvation light can shine throughout the world. Again, I ask for your special grace and anointing to remain consistent so that I can be fit for your earthly and heavenly blessings. For in the name of Jesus Christ I pray. Amen.

8

Eternal Rock of Ages, please give me the grace to faithfully serve you always so that I can qualify for your blessings. Let your benefits be pronounced in my life, so that all people can testify to your goodness. For in the name of Jesus Christ I pray. Amen.

9

Jehovah, please help me to have a good motive and pursue missions that will incur your blessings. Let my thoughts and actions result to the betterment of people's lives. Also, let my efforts glorify your name. Let me succeed in my endeavors, and enable me to share the testimony of your goodness throughout the world. For in the name of Jesus Christ I pray. Amen.

PRAYER OF SELF-CONTROL

Self-control is someone's ability to restrain his feelings, and behave well in the face of trials and impulses. Children of God are asked to exhibit this trait so that God can be glorified in our lives.

"A man without self-control is like a city broken into and left without walls". (Proverbs 25:28 ESV)

---

* * *

Pray for Self-Control

1

Good Lord, please teach me how to apply moderation to everything I do. Do not let me be carried away with worldly activities, but let me be disciplined and have self-control. Let me be efficient in serving you at all times so that you can be happy with me. For in the name of Jesus Christ I pray. Amen.

2

Dear God, please do not let me play with sin. Let me live a holy and acceptable life before you so that I can qualify for your blessings. Please guide me to operate under the leadership of your Holy Spirit so that I can enjoy your goodness throughout the days of my life. For in the name of Jesus Christ I pray. Amen.

3

Dear God, please give me your grace to adequately utilize my tongue. Let my words be seasoned with grace and bless other people. Also, let my speech motivate people to move closer to you. In Jesus Name, I Pray. Amen

PRAYER TO PREACH GOSPEL

This is the final and greatest commission of our Lord Jesus Christ to all Christians. Everyone without exception is required to preach the gospel and populate God's kingdom.

"And he said unto them, Go ye into all the world, and preach the gospel to every creature". (Mark 16:15 KJV)

---

* * *

Pray for Grace to Preach the Gospel

1

Dear God, please release your Holy Spirit upon me so that I can be effective in preaching gospel. Let your Holy Spirit energize me to live a successful life on earth. Let him also guide me to remain fit for your heavenly kingdom. For in the name of Jesus Christ I pray. Amen.

2

In the name of Jesus Christ, I receive the power of God to preach the irresistible gospel. I also claim the strength and grace of God to preach the gospel that will lead sinners to repentance and have access to the kingdom of God. Let the Holy Spirit come upon me, and let him empower me to do exploits for his kingdom. For in the name of Jesus Christ I make my declarations. Amen.

3

Dear Jesus Christ, please help me to be your true ambassador on earth, and help me to effectively preach your gospel to other people. Do not let me be an obstacle to gospel evangelization, but help me to support it and spread further. I also pray for your ministers that spread your gospel throughout the world, please anoint and empower them unto success. Give them grace to irresistibly share your good news and lead people to your kingdom through them. Let every opposing force towards your gospel perish. For in the name of Jesus Christ I pray. Amen.

4

Father, I could not appreciate you enough for all your goodness in my life. I understand that an effective means of demonstrating my gratitude to you is to preach the gospel. Therefore, I ask you to give me the grace to proclaim your good news, so that other people can be saved also. Please fill my mouth with your Holy Spirit and use me as living vessel that is worthy of bearing fruits for your kingdom. For in the name of Jesus Christ I make my requests. Amen.

5

Almighty God, please give me the confidence to preach the gospel at all times. Help me to be firm and determined to preach your good news under whatever condition. Anoint me and make me a useful instrument to harvesting plentiful souls into your kingdom. For in the name of Jesus Christ I pray. Amen.

6

Hallelujah Jesus reigns. He is the source of gospel, and no force on earth can stop his movement. Hallelujah! I am a servant of Jesus Christ who is commissioned to preach the gospel. Since Jesus could not be stopped from achieving his salvation objective, I cannot be stopped from preaching the gospel as well. I am empowered by the Holy Spirit to do exploits for God. I am anointed by Jesus Christ to proclaim gospel from house floors to rooftops. I am anointed to share the good news of Jesus and loot the kingdom of darkness. I am empowered by the Lord to do exploits. Yes, I am anointed by the Lord for the sake of his kingdom! Hallelujah.

7

Dear God, I want to preach your gospel, please teach me how to do so. Give me confidence to share your good news with unbelievers so that they too can become saved. Anoint me to freely extend the light of your gospel to both the reached and unreached parts of the world. Please let your light shine through me so that many people can become saved and qualify for your kingdom. Also, please keep me fit so that I can be counted among people that will meet and rejoice with you on the last day. For in the name of Jesus Christ I pray. Amen.

8

Dear Jesus Christ, I receive your grace and anointing to preach the gospel by faith. Empower me through your Holy Spirit to preach the gospel and expand your kingdom. Let any Satan's effort to frustrate my evangelistic mission fail. Let oppositions against my gospel services be frustrated. Let your Holy Spirit empower me to propagate your gospel on the land; in the sea, and on the air. Let me prosper with your gospel throughout the world. For in the name of Jesus Christ I pray. Amen.

9

Dear Jesus Christ, please anoint me with grace to preach the indispensable gospel. Increase my faith to stand firm with the task of evangelism. Enable me to preach your gospel fearlessly and ceaselessly. Please enable me to be your true ambassador, and let me bring huge rewards to your kingdom. For in the name of Jesus Christ I pray. Amen.

PRAYER FOR BAPTISM OF HOLY SPIRIT

There is no limit to what a believer can do with help from the Holy Spirit. Among others, Holy Spirit empowers, comforts, and teaches his recipients.

"But ye shall receive power, after that the Holy Ghost is come upon you: and ye shall be witnesses unto me both in Jerusalem, and in all Judaea, and in Samaria, and unto the uttermost part of the earth." (Act 1:8 KJV)

---

* * *

Pray for Baptism of the Holy Spirit

1

Father, I understand that no one can be a successful Christian without the help of the Holy Spirit. Please baptize me with your

Holy Spirit as you did to your disciples on the Day of Pentecost. Let your Spirit enable me to make significant positive contributions to other people's lives. Also, let your Holy Spirit teach and guide me into all righteousness so that I can please you well. Let your Spirit enable me to live an overcomer's life on earth, and let me be a partaker of heaven. For in the name of Jesus Christ I pray. Amen.

2

Eternal Rock of Ages, please let your Holy Spirit rule me at all times. Enable me to be sensitive to your leadership, and do not let me satisfy flesh desires. Let me grow in faith, and let your power be demonstrated in my life with significant testimonies. For in the name of Jesus Christ I pray. Amen.

3

Jehovah, I understand that no one can satisfy you in holiness without the power of the Holy Spirit. I also understand that no one can receive the Holy Spirit without accepting Jesus Christ as Lord. Therefore, I confess Jesus Christ as Lord, and I accept him as my personal Savior. Through Christ, I will satisfy God, and I will inherit eternal life. Amen.

4

Dear God, I understand that selfishness must not play any part in my spiritual exercise. I must only demonstrate my spiritual gifts in a way that will benefit my fellow believers and also profit your kingdom. Therefore, I ask for your grace to meet every expectation. Let your Holy Spirit richly dwell in me so that I can take every necessary step required to glorify your name. Empower me to serve you with humility, and please let me be an effective servant that will prosper your kingdom always. At the end of my earthly race, let me enter heaven to receive your imperishable crown of glory. For in the name of Jesus Christ I pray. Amen.

5

Dear God, please help me to demonstrate gifts of the Holy Spirit in a manner that will glorify your name. Let your Holy Spirit operate in me with grace and power to benefit the church and your kingdom! Please keep me humble, and do not let me arrogate your glory unto myself. Let me serve you with fear and trembling; let my services be acceptable in your sight at all time, and let your name be praised forever. For in the name of Jesus Christ I pray. Amen.

6

Dear Jesus Christ, please baptize me with your Holy Spirit so that I can prosper. Let me have your Holy Spirit so that I can effectively evangelize your gospel. Also, let your Holy Spirit empower me to live triumphant life on earth. Please make me an embodiment of your testimony through the help of your Holy Spirit. For in the name of Jesus Christ I pray. Amen.

7

O good Lord, I have realized that Holy Spirit is the key to an effective ministry. Therefore, I pray that you will assist my ministry to operate in the Holy Spirit. Since the Holy Spirit symbolizes your abiding presence, let him dominate my life and ministry so that I can prosper. Also, I pray for other ministers that you will enable them to allow your Holy Spirit to operate in their lives and ministries. Let all Christians who serve you in any capacity – within and without the church setting – operate in the Holy Spirit so that they can prosper. At the end of it all, let your servants be qualified to receive crowns of glory in heaven. For in the name of Jesus Christ I pray. Amen.

8

Dear God, I believe your scripture that states, *"I can do all things through Christ who strengthens me"* (*Philippians 4:13*). Therefore, I ask you to please empower me through the Holy Spirit to be focus, diligent, and hardworking. Let me succeed in all my endeavors, so that I can share your testimony of goodness to other people. For in the name of Jesus Christ I pray. Amen.

9

Father, please help me to consistently study bible and listen to the leadership of the Holy Spirit. Do not let me be lazy in studying your word. Also, let me prayerfully consider every teaching that is presented to me, and give me the grace to reject deceptive teachings. Enable me to accept and celebrate all truth that will liberate me from sin, and make me heavenly bound. Let your word and leadership of the Holy Spirit prosper me now, and always. For in the name of Jesus Christ I pray. Amen.

10

Dear God, please let your Holy Spirit reign in my heart and let him enable me to embrace activities that will earn me your blessings. Mortify all works of the flesh in my life, and let your divine Spirit strengthen me to bear good fruits that lead to your kingdom. For in the name of Jesus Christ I pray. Amen.

11

O Lord, I want to receive the baptism of your Holy Spirit. To qualify for this treasured gift, I confess my sins and repent from them. Please baptize me with your Holy Spirit to be empowered to walk before you in righteousness. Let your Spirit turn me to a giant Christian who will live a triumphant life on earth. Let him enable me with the ability to effectively serve you to bear fruits for your kingdom. Let your divine Spirit guide me in every aspect of life to enjoy your benefits. For in the name of Jesus Christ I pray. Amen

12

Dear Jesus Christ, please help me to exercise my authority reserved in your name. Empower me to subdue all forms and appearances of Goliath in my life. Anoint me with your Holy Spirit to exercise my faith in a manner that will benefit your kingdom, and also prosper my life. For in the name of Jesus Christ I pray. Amen.

13

Dear Lord, *"If you can use anyone, you can use me!"* I am ready for your use. I let down my pride and I release myself for your use. I will not be rebellious to you anymore, and I will do whatever you ask me to do. I will jump if you say jump, and I will sit if you say sit. I will stop questioning your authority again, but I will completely yield myself to you. Please use me today, tomorrow, and throughout the days of my life. For in the name of Jesus Christ I pray. Amen.

14

Dear Jesus, please use me! I understand that you will bless me if I make myself available for your use; therefore, I am determined to release myself for your use. Henceforth, I will gladly do whatever you ask me to do, and I will do it effectively. Please showcase your grace and power through my obedience, and let me prosper in my commissions. For in the name of Jesus Christ I pray. Amen.

GRACE TO ABSTAIN FROM SEXUAL SIN

S exual sin includes not only sexual intercourse but also other sexual activities that are outside of God-approved marriage between a man and a woman. Sex is not only a matter for the body but also a matter of the mind. The Bible affirmed:

> *"...It is God's will that you keep away from sexual sin as a mark of your devotion to him..."* (I Thessalonians 4:3 GNT)

In its proper context of marriage, sex is a good thing as the scripture stated,

> *"A man will leave his father and mother and be united to his wife, and they will become one flesh"* (Gen. 2:24 KJV)

* * *

Pray to Abstain from Sexual Sin

1

Dear God, please save me from sexual sins. Help me to consciously resist sexual sins. Empower me to be disciplined and say no to all sexual temptations. Help me to live a pure and acceptable life before you at all times, so that I can obtain your benefits on earth and in heaven also. For in the name of Jesus Christ I pray. Amen.

2

Dear God, I realized that it is foolishness to mistake your love for sexual immorality. Your love is not selfish, and it does not seek carnal satisfactions. Therefore, I ask you to give me the grace to abstain from sexual sin, and pursue a pure relationship with you. Please do not let me yield to the temptations of Satan and fall into sexual sins. I receive your grace and empowerment of the Holy Spirit to live a pure life and satisfy you on earth so that I can inherit your eternal kingdom. For in the name of Jesus Christ I pray. Amen.

3

Father, I know that I am not perfect and I have transgressed against your will. I have decided to amend my ways before you; from now on, I will serve you with purity, and I will obey your instructions. I will stop my sexual sins, and I will serve you in holiness. I am asking for grace and empowerment of your Holy Spirit so that I can remain focused and keep serving you in holiness. Please keep me fit for the rapture, and let your faithful testimony remain in my mouth. For in the name of Jesus Christ I pray. Amen.

4

Holy Spirit, please save me from sexual sins; create in me a clean heart and renew a right spirit within me! I am sorry for all my past sins. I am sorry for every sexual sin that I have committed. Please help me to have a fresh start with you. Let me serve you with the beauty of your holiness, and let me walk uprightly with you at all time. Let your Holy Spirit keep me fit for your second coming. Please, write my name in the book of life, and let me qualify to partake in your heavenly banquette. For in the name of Jesus Christ I pray. Amen.

5

Everlasting God, I understand that sexual sin is an abomination to you; therefore, I want to stop the practice in my life. I am sorry for those sexual sins that I have committed in the past, I am now determined to live a holy life before you. I will not entertain sexual sin anymore! From now on, I will abstain from anything that can corrupt my mind; I will stop all my immoral activities. I will be conscious of holiness, and I will do my best to practice it. Please fill me with your Holy Spirit, and empower me to do the right thing at all time. At the end of my earthly race, let me be awarded your medal of honor in heaven for standing uprightly with you. For in the name of Jesus Christ I pray. Amen.

6

Jehovah, please I do not want my soul to burn in hell fire, but I want to make heaven! Help me to resist sins; do not let me yield to temptations, but empower me to maintain my body in holiness so that I can receive your positive rewards in heaven. For in the name of Jesus Christ I pray. Amen.

PRAYER FOR HAPPY HOME

Marriage is the permanent commitment of spouses that come from either similar or different backgrounds. Marriage is to be enjoyed, and not endured. Couples must strive to achieve happy Christian home - Specially through prayers. The Bible says:

"For the husband is the head of the wife, even as Christ is the head of the church: and he is the savior of the body. Therefore, as the church is subject unto Christ, so let the wives be to their own husbands in everything. Husbands, love your wives, even as Christ also loved the church, and gave himself for it; That he might sanctify and cleanse it with the washing of water by the word, That he might present it to himself a glorious church, not having spot, or wrinkle, or any such thing; but that it should be holy and without blemish. So ought men to love their wives as their own bodies. He that loveth his wife loveth himself. For no man ever yet hated his own flesh; but nourisheth and cherisheth it, even as the Lord the church: For

we are members of his body, of his flesh, and of his bones. For this cause shall a man leave his father and mother, and shall be joined unto his wife, and they two shall be one flesh. This is a great mystery: but I speak concerning Christ and the church. Nevertheless, let every one of you in particular so love his wife even as himself; and the wife sees that she reverence her husband." (*Ephesians 5: 22-33 KJV*)

---

* * *

Pray to Achieve Happy Home

1

Dear God, please let there be genuine love in my marriage. Help us (me and my spouse) to have sacrificial love for each other. Let my marriage love represent the type of sacrificial love that you have demonstrated for saving humanity. Let love, joy, understanding, and assurance of salvation reign supremely in our home. For in the name of Jesus Christ I pray. Amen.

2

Dear God, I pray that you will bless every marriage throughout the world. I also pray for the prospective husbands and wives, please help them to make right decisions in their marriage choices. Bless bachelors and spinsters with their perfect "bones and flesh." Let all Christian marriages enjoy your due benefits on earth. For in the name of Jesus Christ I pray. Amen.

3

Dear God, please help me to express true love to my family. Let me be your true ambassador in my home so that your name can be glorified. Help me to be a godly husband, wife, child, or grandchild. Let me be a godly niece, nephew, and cousin to promote your gospel light in my family. For in the name of Jesus Christ I pray. Amen.

PRAYER OF STEADFASTNESS

C hristians must be established in faith since we have been made right with God through faith in Jesus Christ. We must not satisfy the wish of Satan, but resist him. We must recognize who we are in Christ and remain steadfast.

"Rooted and built up in him, strengthened in the faith as you were taught, and overflowing with thankfulness."(Colossians 2:7 NIV)

"For he hath made him to be sin for us, who knew no sin; that we might be made the Righteousness of God in him." (2 Corinthians 5:21 KJV)

Pray for Steadfast Faith

1

Dear Jesus Christ, please help me to remain steadfast in faith so that I can be crowned in heaven. Empower me through your Holy Spirit to be diligent and keep your testimony until the end. When the end comes, let me receive a warm welcome in heaven, and let me partake in your holy banquette. Amen.

2

I thank the Almighty God for creating me in his image. I appreciate him for giving me his spirit and a soul. I really thank God for creating me a human being and giving me dominion over other things that he created. All I ask my God is to give me the ability to satisfy him with my life. I plead for God's grace and mercy to comply with his desires so that I can always be recognized as a grateful child. May the grace of the Almighty God sufficient for me now and always! For in the name of Jesus Christ I pray. Amen.

3

Eternal Rock of Ages, please give me strength to overcome sin. Give me the grace to resist temptations, and help me to live uprightly with you always. Enable me to exercise genuine repentance so that I can be fit for your kingdom. For in the name of Jesus Christ I pray. Amen.

4

Dear God, please give me the grace to walk in dignity before you. Give me the ability to desist from anything that can cause me to sin against you. Help me to use accurate judgment, and let your Holy Spirit guide me into all righteousness so that I can be fit for your kingdom. For in the name of Jesus Christ I pray. Amen.

5

O Lord, please help me to serve you at all times with undivided attention, and let me faithfully direct my praises and prayers towards you always. Help me to remain consistent with you throughout the days of my life. For in the name of Jesus Christ I pray. Amen.

6

Father, please keep my feet from falling but help me to hold firm to teachings that have validation in the bible. Do not let me become complacent with your word but help me to abide by your instructions so that I can prosper. Give me the gift of discernment of spirit so that I can hold firm to the truth always. For in the name of Jesus Christ I pray. Amen.

7

Dear God, please give me the grace to be a diligent Christian who is dedicated to good works, and also responsible for family and society. Bless my positive efforts and reward my labors with fruitfulness. For in the name of Jesus Christ I pray. Amen.

8

Almighty God, please teach me how to love and fear you always. Let me apply your fear to whatever I do so that I can prosper. Assist me to overcome temptations, and energize me to do works of righteousness, so that I can enjoy your benefits throughout the days of my life. For in the name of Jesus Christ I pray. Amen.

9

Dear loving God, my goals and aspirations are to satisfy you with holy living so that I can qualify for your eternal kingdom. Help me to genuinely repent from my sins, and empower me to improve my relationship with you. Anoint me with grace to spend the rest of my life in a way that satisfies you. Let me walk uprightly before you, and let your Holy Spirit richly dwell in me so that I can remain rapturable! For in the name of Jesus Christ I pray. Amen.

10

Dear God, please give me your strength to remain a steadfast Christian. Enable me to keep irresistible faith in the time of persecution. Strengthen my mind not to fall into Satan's temptations. Empower me through your Holy Spirit to live an acceptable life before you always, so that I can receive your benefits in this world and in heaven also. For in the name of Jesus Christ I pray. Amen.

11

I pray that God establishes my heart to be steadfast and not be moved by any windstorm of persecution or attack. May the Lord Jesus Christ keep me safe until the day of his second coming when he will transport all saints to his heavenly home? May he count me worthy to receive his imperishable crown of glory, and may he decorate my life with beauty and honor forever! For in the name of Jesus Christ I pray. Amen.

12

Glory to God for Jesus Christ has brought permanent deliverance for his people! I am determined to serve Jesus because he has died for my sins and resurrected to give me eternal life. Since I am now a child of God, sin, death, and hell do not have power over me anymore. Glory to God, Hallelujah!

PRAYER FOR GENUINE LOVE OF GOD

G od's love for mankind is undeserved and unfailing: He loves us despite our weaknesses. This unconditional love of God was revealed on the cross when Jesus Christ died for our sins.

"Then said Jesus, Father, forgive them; for they know not what they do."(Luke 23:43KJV)

---

* * *

Pray for Genuine Love of God

1

Father, please flourish my heart with genuine love that will benefit other people and me. Also, let the demonstrations of my love result to the glorification of your name. Let my love be selfless, impartial, truthful, and fruitful! For in the name of Jesus Christ I pray. Amen.

2

Dear God, please help me to love you more than silver and gold. Enable me to freely give you my best offerings. Let me freely give without grudges. Let me be appreciative enough to offer you tangible offerings that will incur your rare blessings into my life. For in the name of Jesus Christ I pray. Amen.

3

Dear God, I ask that you please grant me the grace to forgive people that have offended me. Empower me to exercise forgiveness - even when it is not convenient. Do not let me take laws into my hands, but allow you to handle matters in a way that will glory your holy name. For in the name of Jesus Christ I make my requests. Amen.

PRAYER AGAINST UNHOLY RELATIONSHIP

"*E*vil *communication corrupts good manner!*" (*1 Corinthians 15:33*). Children of God must be mindful of the relationships that we keep. A relationship can interfere positively or negatively with our walk with God. An interaction that can lead us into any form of disobedience to God must be avoided at all cost.

This then is the message which we have heard of him, and declare unto you, that God is light, and in him is no darkness at all. If we say that we have fellowship with him, and walk in darkness, we lie, and do not the truth: But if we walk in the light, as he is in the light, we have fellowship one with another, and the blood of Jesus Christ his Son cleanseth us from all sin. If we say that we have no sin, we deceive ourselves, and the truth is not in us. If we confess our sins, he is faithful and just to forgive us our sins, and to cleanse us from all unrighteousness. If we say that we have not sinned, we make him a liar, and his word is not in us". (1 John 1:5-10 KJV)

---

* * *

Pray against Unholy Relationship

1

Dear God, I realized that illicit relationships are ungodly and they can make anybody fall from grace, therefore, I ask you to please help me to maintain sanctity as a single (or married) person. Help me to abstain from any interaction that may damage my relationship with you. Please let me be holy and faithfully serve you so that I can enjoy your benefits, and so that I can prosper in all aspects of life. For in the name of Jesus Christ I pray. Amen.

2

O Good Lord, I am sorry for every immoral sin that I have committed. I understand that my body is the temple of the Holy Spirit; I am determined to shun fornication and idolatry. From now on, I will maintain purity as a true child of God, and I will maintain a consistent relationship with you always. Please give me strength and grace to remain steadfast with you unto the end. For in the name of Jesus Christ I pray. Amen.

3

Dear God, please give me the grace to live a holy life before you. Do not let me yield to temptations of sin, but enable me with grace to stand uprightly and walk faithfully before you always. Let your Holy Spirit empower me to faithfully run my Christian race in a way that will glorify your name, and also make me qualify for your kingdom. Please count me worthy now and always! For in the name of Jesus Christ I pray. Amen.

PRAYER FOR DISCERNMENT OF SPIRITS

The gift of discernment of spirits is one of the gifts of the Holy Spirit (*1 Corinthians 12:4-11*). It is given by the Holy Spirit to profit God's kingdom. This rare gift will enable a believer to have better understanding of any matter beyond a literal sense.

"Watch and pray so that you will not fall into temptation. The spirit is willing, but the flesh is weak" (Matthew 26:41 NIV).

---

* * *

Pray to Possess Discerning Spirit

1

O Lord, please teach me how to respond to the leadership of the Holy Spirit. Let me be prayerful and sensitive, so that I can understand every instruction that the Spirit offers. Make me a sensitive servant that listen to the voice of the Holy Spirit, and make me an obedient servant that yields to his instructions. Let my obedience benefit your kingdom. Let me never regret serving you, but help me to prosper in this life, and in heaven also. For in the name of Jesus Christ I pray. Amen.

2

Dear God, please guide my steps not to seek counsels from ungodly people. Assist me to seek godly counselors who may guide me into making right decisions. Help me to prayerfully consider any counsel before I take an action. Do not let me rush into judgment and regret afterward. Rather, let your Holy Spirit counsel, comfort, and empower me to appropriately make decisions that will result in positive benefits. For in the name of Jesus Christ I pray. Amen.

3

Father, please guide my footsteps so that I do not sin against you. Do not let me sin against you, so that Satan will not have an advantage over me. Empower me through your Holy Spirit to obey all your commandments, and help me to faithfully serve you so that I can prosper throughout the days of my life. For in the name of Jesus Christ I pray. Amen.

PRAYER OF SALVATION

The gospel of Jesus Christ is free for everyone, and anyone can have it at any time. Ideally, due to human sins, no one is worthy of free salvation given through gospel; however, Christ has made it free for us! Hence, all people should maximize their opportunity of salvation to become a child of God. The process of obtaining salvation is very simple. For anyone to be saved, he or she must confess Jesus Christ as Lord through faith. The scripture explained the process:

"...That if thou shalt confess with thy mouth the Lord Jesus, and shalt believe in thine heart that God hath raised him from the dead, thou shalt be saved. For with the heart man believeth unto righteousness; and with the mouth confession is made unto salvation" (Romans 10:9 -10 KJV).

* * *

Pray the Prayer of Salvation

1

Dear Jesus Christ, what a wonderful savior you are to suffer persecutions and death for the sake of saving my soul! I understand that you have paid the debt of my sins in full through your resurrection power. Therefore, I declare my faith in you that you are Jesus Christ, the Son of God! I confess you as my Lord, and I accept you as my personal Savior. Henceforth, I will serve you with all my heart, and I will faithfully follow you throughout the days of my life. So, help me God! Amen.

2

Dear Jesus Christ, I understand that you are the Son of God, and you are the one capable of saving people's soul. Therefore, I confess you as my personal Lord and Savior. I am determined to serve you for the rest of my life. Please give me the grace to keep serving you, so that I can inherit the gift of eternal life. Amen.

3

Dear God, please give me your enablement to always worship you with meaningful purpose. Let my actions come from a pure a heart; let my continuous prayers, praises, and offerings be acceptable in your presence. Enable me to serve you sincerely and consistently throughout the days of my life, so that I can have an abiding prosperity. For in the name of Jesus Christ I pray. Amen.

4

Dear Jesus Christ, I cannot pretend that I do not understand the amazing work of salvation that you have accomplished for me through your death and resurrection. You have died for my sins and you have given me eternal life. You have also promised to bless me with your Holy Spirit so that I would be able to effectively preach your gospel. Therefore, I release myself for you today, and I accept you Jesus Christ as my personal Lord and Savior. I also ask for your Holy Spirit's empowerment that will enable me to effectively preach your gospel. Please grant me grace and let me remain your true child unto the end. For in the name of Jesus Christ I pray. Amen.

5

Dear God, I have learned that salvation of Jesus Christ is as simple as "ABC," therefore, I declare my faith in him (Jesus Christ) today. I confess Jesus as Lord, and I accept him as my personal savior. I confess that he is the Son of God and I will serve him from now on, and for the rest of my life. I believe that I am now saved. Glory to God. Hallelujah, Amen.

6

Everlasting Father, please help me to understand the fact that salvation is received by grace through faith in Jesus Christ. Help me to live the rest of my life celebrating the free gift of salvation that I have received. Please keep me in the joy of salvation, and I will serve you for the rest of my life. For in the name of Jesus Christ I pray. Amen.

7

Dear God, I praise your name for adopting me as your son/daughter through my confession of faith in Jesus Christ. I praise you for changing my status from "slavery" to "sonship." Since my confession in Jesus Christ, I have become a child of God, and my name has been written in the book of life. Praise God heaven is my home. I commit my life to you today, tomorrow, and forevermore! Thank you, Jesus Christ, for your saving grace. Amen.

8

O Lord, I have a desire to serve you in holiness; I want to meet your expectations and live a holy life. Meanwhile, it is sometimes difficult to meet your holiness standard; therefore, I am asking for your special grace to measure up. Empower me through your Holy Spirit to do what pleases you, so that I can be qualified to enter your kingdom. In addition, I understand that no one can make it to heaven without first confessing Jesus Christ as Lord. Therefore, I confess your Son Jesus Christ as my personal Lord and Savior. I will follow him today, and throughout my life - so help me God. Amen.

9

Loving Father, I understand that heaven and hell are real places; my choice is to go to heaven and not hell fire. Therefore, I confess my faith in Jesus Christ today. I declare him as Lord, and I accept him into my life as my personal Savior. My total life belongs to Jesus Christ; I will serve him throughout the days of my life. Amen.

10

Dear Jesus Christ, I want to go to heaven since hell fire would be too hot for my likening. Let me go to heaven so that I can live in beautiful mansions and enjoy a peaceful atmosphere. I am making my confessions today: I believe that Jesus Christ is the Son of God, and I confess him as my personal Lord and Savior. I give Jesus my complete heart, and I promise to serve him throughout the days of my life. I renounce the devil and all his evil works. I confess all my sins and I forsake them. Henceforth, I am a born again Christian and I will remain so for the rest of my life. Amen.

11

Ancient of Days, please help me to understand the fact that salvation is received by grace through faith in Jesus Christ. Help me to live the rest of my life celebrating the free gift of salvation that I have received. Please keep me in the joy of salvation, and I will serve you for the rest of my life. For in the name of Jesus Christ I pray. Amen.

PRAYER FOR SPIRITUAL GROWTH

Spiritual growth is God's unique blessing for his children. He matures believers in wisdom and power to conform to his standard of righteousness, so that we can serve him with deep devotion and be fit for his kingdom. The Bible says

---

"But grow in grace, and in the knowledge of our Lord and Savior, Jesus Christ. To Him be glory both now and forever. Amen." (2 Peters 3:18 NIV)

---

* * *

Pray for Spiritual Growth

1

Almighty Father, I do not want to be a baby Christian anymore; I want to take Christianity seriously! Please anoint me to stand upright with you. Let me hold firm to my confession of Jesus Christ. Take away every persecution that the enemies may hurl against me. Empower me through your Holy Spirit to remain undefeatable, and anoint me to preach your gospel throughout the world. Let my outreaches touch people's lives and lead them to the salvation of your Son Jesus Christ. At the end of my earthly journey, let me hear your favorable statement "Weldon and welcome my good servant!" For in the name of Jesus Christ I pray. Amen.

2

Jehovah, please let me grow up and become a mature Christian. Enable me to take Christianity seriously, and help me to be committed to it. Let me be consistent in my relationship with you, and let me please you in all my endeavors. Also, give me boldness to preach your gospel and represent you well on earth. Let me serve you well to qualify for your imperishable crown of glory in heaven. For in the name of Jesus Christ I pray. Amen.

3

O Good Lord, please enable me to demonstrate a positive attitude towards correction. Give me contrite, teachable, and humble spirit. Keep me honest, and help me to admit my mistakes. Enable me to take positive steps toward improvement, and help me to be a growing Christian who prioritizes holiness, honesty, and integrity above other virtues. Please do these and much more for me! For in the name of Jesus Christ I pray. Amen.

4

Almighty God, please help me to study the bible (which is your word) always. Enable me with grace to stay consistent with your word so that I can gain knowledge and wisdom needed to live a successful life on earth, and also to be counted worthy to enter your eternal kingdom. For in the name of Jesus Christ I pray. Amen.

PRAYER OF DEDICATION

God desires that his children are dedicated into faithfully serving him. He does not expect us to keep casual relationship with him. As we devote our time and services to him, great and mighty works of God will manifest in our lives.

"Yet a time is coming and has now come when the true worshipers will worship the Father in the Spirit and in truth, for they are the kind of worshipers the Father seeks. God is spirit, and his worshipers must worship in the Spirit and in truth" (John 4:23-24 NIV).

---

* * *

Pray the Prayer of Dedication

1

Father, please let me adequately live my life for you. Help me to devote the early stage of my life into your faithful services. Enable me to utilize my time, energy, knowledge, finances, and other resources for your services. Let me wholly commit my life to you and your services, so that your kingdom can be populated. Please let my services be acceptable before you, and let me receive your over-whelming blessings throughout the days of my life. For in the name of Jesus Christ I pray. Amen.

2

Jehovah, please I want to go to heaven where there shall be perfect joy. This world is not perfect, and hell fire would be worse! The only choice I prefer is heaven! Please count me worthy for heaven. I understand that Jesus Christ is the only sure way to heaven; a person who believes and follows him will make it on the last day. Therefore, I confess Jesus Christ as my personal Lord and Savior. I will serve him from now on, and forever. I confess my sins and repent from them. I have determined to start afresh with you in holiness and integrity. Please let me remain heavenly bound. For I have obtained my salvation by grace through faith in the name of your Son Jesus Christ. Amen.

3

Dear Jesus Christ, Hell Fire is too hot and I do not want to go there – neither do I want it to become my permanent home! I want to go to heaven that has peaceful bliss – where people never suffer pain or abuse. Hell has horror but heaven has peace! Therefore, I am deter-mined to invest my future and destiny in you so that I can go to heaven. Today, I am determined to sign up for your life insurance program that will never fail: I confess you Jesus Christ as my personal Lord and Savior, and I give you my complete life forever. Henceforth, I will serve you with all my heart, and I will share my salvation experience with other people. So help me God. Amen.

4

Dear God, I am determined to commit my total life into your service; I will serve you always. Please give me your grace and empowerment to faithfully follow you, so that I can prosper in all my ways. Please give me all it takes to remain your true child forever! For in the name of Jesus Christ I pray. Amen.

5

Ancient of Days, I understand that I cannot deceive you with pretense and eye-service. I also acknowledge the fact that you will bless me if I faithfully serve you. Therefore, I ask that you give me the grace to commit my total heart to serving you. Please let me qualify for your blessing. For in the name of Jesus Christ I pray. Amen.

6

Dear Jesus Christ, I believe that you died for my sins, and resurrected to give me the gift of eternal life. I confess my sins and repent from them. I declare you as the Lord of my life, and I will forever serve you. Please write my name in the Book of Life, so that I can be qualified to enjoy your eternal blessings in heaven. For in the name of Jesus Christ I pray. Amen.

7

Dear God, please enable me to focus my services to you only. Do not let me serve idols, and do not let me share your glory with someone else. Let my total heart be committed to you throughout the days of my life, so that I can enjoy your benefits on earth and in heaven. For in the name of Jesus Christ I pray. Amen.

8

Dear Jesus Christ, I confess that you are the Son of God who died for the sins of the world. You have died and resurrected to give me eternal life, therefore, I confess you as my personal Lord and Savior. I offer you my entire life, and I will serve you throughout the days of my life. Please write my name in the book of life, and let me qualify to rejoice with you in heaven. For in the name of Jesus Christ I pray. Amen.

9

Dear Father, how awesome you are! You are the best thing that has ever happened to me. You are my God, my rock, and my fortress! My total life is dedicated to you. Since you are God that is the same yesterday, today, and forever, I claim all your promises of blessings mentioned in the scriptures. May the riches of Abraham abide by me! May the prosperity of Joseph become my portion, and may the victory of David become my testimony! Since I am a child of God, may his divine favor, riches, and goodness follow me all the days of my life. May all my prayers and heart meditations be granted through the name of Jesus Christ. Amen.

10

Father, I believe that Jesus Christ is your only Son sent to save the world. Through him, I receive salvation and gift of eternal life, since there is no other name under heaven through which anyone can be saved. I swear my allegiance to Jesus Christ, and I am determined to serve him throughout the days of my life - so help me God! Amen.

11

Dear God, please help me to dedicate my complete life unto you, and let me serve you with honesty. Enable me to satisfy you with everything I have, and let me be counted worthy to receive your blessings on earth and in heaven also. For in the name of Jesus Christ I pray. Amen.

12

Jehovah, please use me for your glory. Give me a humble heart, and let me be usable for your kingdom. Once, I am used, do not let me arrogate your glory to myself, but help me to direct people's attention to you. Please keep me fit for your kingdom, and let me receive your glorious crown at the end. For in the name of Jesus Christ I pray. Amen.

13

Oh Good Lord, I am committed to dedicating my life to serving you in holiness; therefore, I am determined to give all it takes to stay away from sins - for especially, sexual sins that corrupt body, mind, and soul. Please help me to keep my body pure by resisting fornication and adultery. Help me to maintain the integrity and stay consistent with bible standard. Let me remain pure before you so that I can receive your blessings in this life and in heaven also. For in the name of Jesus Christ I pray. Amen.

14

God, please make me a spiritual person so that I can effectively serve you. Please silence all works of the flesh in my life so that I can enjoy all your benefits. For in the name of Jesus Christ I pray. Amen.

15

Holy Spirit, I am sorry for how I have mishandled my body. I now realize that my body is your temple, and I must not corrupt it. Therefore, I will preserve my body for your glory. Please help me to remain conscious that you will judge all indecent activity. Assist me to maintain my body's sanctity so that I will not be condemned in your presence on Judgment day. Empower me to maintain a faithful and consistent relationship with you throughout the days of my life, so that I can enter your kingdom. For in the name of Jesus Christ I pray. Amen.

16

Father, I ask you to please give me a heart that is sold out for your faithful services. Help me to dedicate my life to serving you with a consistent mind, so that I can receive your rewards of blessing and honor on earth and in heaven. For in the name of Jesus Christ I pray. Amen.

PRAYER OF THANKSGIVING

Thanksgiving is the act of showing gratitude to God for all his good deeds. Christians must offer thanksgiving to God because he dwells in it. The Bible says:

"Enter into his gates with thanksgiving, and into his courts with praise: be thankful unto him, and bless his name. For the LORD is good; his mercy is everlasting; and his truth endureth to all generations". (Psalm 100:4-5 NIV)

* * *

Pray the Prayer of Thanksgiving

1

Father, you deserve every honor in my life. You deserve praises and offering of thanksgiving at all times. No one else can offer me protections and provisions like you do! You have sheltered and cared for me in the time of needs, and you have given me peace during crisis. Why then should I not praise you? Please give me the grace to appreciate you from the bottom of my heart at all times. Do not let me share any part of your glory. Help me to praise you always, and help me to testify to your goodness throughout the world. Also, let my testimony abide so that I can continue to bring praises to your holy name. For in the name of Jesus Christ I pray. Amen.

2

Dear Jesus Christ, what an awesome Lord you are! You sacrificed your life to save my soul! I will praise you from now on. I will sing, dance, and proclaim your goodness throughout the earth. I am determined to shun self-praise but give you due honor throughout the days of my life. So, help me God! Amen.

3

I ask you, God, to please grant me grace and ability to praise you from the bottom of my heart. Let me continue to praise you until I breathe my last breath on earth. Let the testimony of your goodness fill my mouth forever. For in the name of Jesus Christ I pray. Amen.

4

I thank you God for you are the Lord of lords and God of gods! I praise you with every breath that I take. Everything within me says "Thank you!" My praises shall ever come to you. I will praise you in the morning, afternoon, and evening. I will shout the praises of your name throughout the earth. All that I ask from you is grace and strength to continue praising your holy name throughout the days of my life. For in the name of Jesus Christ I pray. Amen.

5

Dear Jesus Christ, I understand that you are the Son of God, and you are the one capable of saving people's soul. Therefore, I confess you as my personal Lord and Savior. I am determined to serve you for the rest of my life. Please give me the grace to keep serving you, so that I can inherit the gift of eternal life. Amen!

6

I love you God for all the signs and wonders that you have performed for humanity. I thank you especially for all your goodness in my life! Thank you for the beauty of every day that I witness. Thank you for sun, moon, sky, and stars. Thank you for fresh air, and thank you for other wonderful natures that you have created. Thank you for yesterday and today; thank you for tomorrow also. Thank you for every benefit that you have brought into my life. I will praise you with everything I have, and I will continue to praise you as long as I live. The praises of your goodness will never elude my mouth - for I will praise you forever more. For in the name of your only Son Jesus Christ I offer all my praises. Amen.

7

I praise you God for you are so good to the people that you have created. Your goodness towards people are immeasurable, therefore, I appreciate you. I ask that you continue to enlighten my heart to recognize your goodness so that I can praise you more. For in the name of Jesus Christ I pray. Amen.

8

Father, please let my mouth be filled with your praises. Give me the ability to recount your goodness in my life, and let my testimony turn into motivation for serving you more. For I pray in the name of Jesus Christ. Amen.

9

I praise you God for you are so good to the people that you have created. Your goodness towards people are immeasurable, therefore, I appreciate you. I ask that you continue to enlighten my heart to recognize your goodness so that I can praise you more. For in the name of Jesus Christ I pray. Amen.

10

Please grant me a grateful heart always, and let your praises never leave my mouth. Empower me to praise you today, tomorrow, and forever. Let heaven recognize me as a beacon of praise to your holy name now and forevermore! For in the name of Jesus Christ I pray. Amen.

11

Father, please teach me how to praise you genuinely. In fact, I will start to praise you from this moment! I will praise you for all your benefits in my life: You have brought me from miry clay and set my feet upon the rock. You have given me new songs and have decorated my life with multiple blessings. I will loudly shout the praise of your name; I will praise you from coast to coast, and I will testify to your goodness always. Please help me to remain grateful to you for all your kindness, and let me ever be a beacon of praise to your name. For in the name of Jesus Christ I pray. Amen.

12

Dear God, how wonder a Father you are! You love me deeply, and you have shown me your loving-kindness. The list of your goodness in my life is endless! You forgave my sins and made me your son/daughter. You fed me when I was hungry, you healed me when I was sick, and you lifted me up when I was down! How can I forget your goodness in my life? I will never forget, but I will be grateful always. Please let your songs of praises ever be in mouth. For in the name of your only Son Jesus Christ I brought you my thanksgiving offering. Amen.

PRAYER OF GODLY LEADERSHIP

C hristians are called to be leaders. If for no other reason, we are to "lead" people to Christ through the examples we live out. A spouse, manager, or any other in position of authority is classified as a leader. All leaders in any capacity are expected to reflect godliness in their leadership positions. The Bible says:

"Therefore I exhort first of all that supplications, prayers, intercessions, and giving of thanks be made for all men, for kings and all who are in authority, that we may lead a quiet and peaceable life in all godliness and reverence. For this is good and acceptable in the sight of God our Savior" (1 Timothy 2:1-3). (Acts 20:28 KJV)

---

* * *

Pray for Godly Leadership Ability

1

Everlasting God, please help me to manage my position in a fashion that will glorify you. Help me to care for people and have your fear in my heart. Let me lead by example and let me motivate people to behave well and please you in their endeavors. Do not let me be carried away with any honor that is associated with my position, and sin against you. Let me serve you well, and let me serve people well. Let my leadership style benefit everyone under my command. For in the name of Jesus Christ I pray. Amen.

2

Lord, please teach me how to offer quality services to you so that I can be fit for your blessings. Also, please enable brothers and sisters in Christ with grace to pursue good courses that will promote your name. Let brethren engage in activities that will populate your kingdom and depopulate Satan's kingdom. Let the church be inspired by the Holy Spirit to serve you with honesty and integrity; keep them fit for your blessings so that unbelievers can witness your goodness in your children's lives and be challenged to serve you also. For in the name of Jesus Christ I pray. Amen.

3

Jehovah, I understand that your goodness will abide by people that honor you; therefore, please teach me how to honor you throughout the days of my life. Let me offer services and worship that will incur your blessings. Let your glory shine upon me so that all people can witness it and glorify your holy name. Please make me a pacesetter of your glory, so that people can be challenged to praise you! For in the name of Jesus Christ I pray. Amen.

4

Father, please make me a good Christian, and let me be a good example for other people to follow. Help me not to be a stumbling block for other people's grace and salvation. Let me faithfully and carefully serve you so that other people can witness this and glorify your holy name. For in the name of Jesus Christ I pray. Amen.

5

Dear God, please give me the grace to pursue righteous riches that will last a lifetime. Give me the grace to follow the righteous path, and not envy wicked people. Let my services be acceptable before you, and let me receive your blessings in this present life, and in heaven also. For in the name of Jesus Christ I pray. Amen.

6

Father, please help me not to keep any ungodly relationship, but help me to maintain a relationship with godly people. Enable me to appreciate Christian values and practice them. Empower me through your Holy Spirit to keep relationships that respect your commandments. Do not let me follow bad examples, but help me to be faithful to you so that I can be fit to receive your blessings always. For in the name of Jesus Christ I pray. Amen.

PRAYER OF BENEVOLENCE

Any act of kindness that a believer extends to other people would be deemed important to God. Christians are to represent God by showing kindness towards others. The Lord will turn our charitable efforts into meeting people's needs; he will also bless us in return. The Bible says,

---

"Give, and it shall be given unto you; good measure, pressed down, and shaken together, and running over, shall men give into your bosom. For with the same measure that ye mete withal it shall be measured to you again."(Luke 6:38 KJV)

---

* * *

Pray the Prayer of Benevolence

1

O Lord God, please keep brothers and sisters in Christ together in the unity of spirit. Let brethren in Christ work together as a theme. Let us evangelize gospel together, and let us sing your praises together. Let us care and assist our fellows who are in need. Enable us to offer prayers and moral support as needed in Jesus Name I Pray. Amen.

2

Also, let us utilize our resources to assist our brethren who are in need. Let your love be paramount in Christian folds so that unbelievers can be challenged to serve you also. Moreover, all Christians are passionately expecting the coming of your Son Jesus Christ; we are expecting his rapture to transport us to heaven where there shall be perfect love and tranquility. Love you, God! For in the name of Jesus Christ I pray. Amen.

3

Dear God, please enable me to demonstrate selfless love towards other people. Do not let me seek selfish gains, but help me to care with a liberal heart. I know that you will definitely bless me if I represent you well on earth, so help me to please you. Let me be your true ambassador on earth, and let me qualify to receive your heavenly rewards. For in the name of Jesus Christ I make my requests. Amen.

PRAYER OF DEVOTION

God wants us to engage in devotional practices that will draw us closer to him. Our practices will also turn to become spiritual nourishments for our souls. The Bible says:

"No servant can serve two masters: for either he will hate the one, and love the other; or else he will hold to the one, and despise the other. Ye cannot serve God and mammon..." (Luke 16 vs13 KJV)

---

* * *

Pray the Prayer of Devotion

1

Heavenly Lord, please help me to seek your face in prayers and obey your instructions so that I can prosper. Enable me to trust that you are in charge of my life, and nothing can alter your original plans for me. Let me carefully listen to you, and let me faithfully obey you so that I can succeed and have an abiding testimony. For in the name of Jesus Christ I pray. Amen.

2

Jehovah, please help me to consistently study bible and listen to the leadership of the Holy Spirit. Do not let me be lazy in studying your word. Also, let me prayerfully consider every teaching that is presented to me, and give me the grace to reject deceptive teachings. Enable me to accept and celebrate all truth that will liberate me from sin, and make me heavenly bound. Let your word and leadership of the Holy Spirit prosper me now, and always. For in the name of Jesus Christ I pray. Amen.

3

Dear God, please teach me how to offer you honest sacrifice. Let my efforts and sacrifice of praise come with an open mind. Do not let me hold back, but let me use my resources to honor you liberally, so that I can be qualified to obtain your favor always. For in the name of Jesus Christ I pray. Amen.

4

O Lord, please let your fire of evangelism burn in me. Empower me to ceaselessly proclaim your gospel so that unbelievers can come to the knowledge of your Son Jesus Christ. As I preach, let people respond. Give them the grace to change their mind so that they can escape the punishment of hell, but be qualified for the blessings of heaven. Please keep your people fit for your kingdom. For in the name of Jesus Christ I pray. Amen.

5

Able God, please give me the grace to serve you with fear and humility. Help me to follow your instructions and yield to your corrections. Guide me through your Holy Spirit so that my decisions can satisfy you always. Let me always qualify for your blessing. For in the name of Jesus Christ I pray. Amen.

6

Everlasting Father, I want to be a devout Christian, to daily study your word, and apply every necessary lesson to my life. Please help me to understand the principles of the bible; enable me to comply with your laws, and help me to maintain a consistent relationship with you. Help me to be an honest Christian, and bless me for every positive effort that I make to satisfy you. Give me the grace to remain a devout Christian throughout the days of my life. For in the name of Jesus Christ I pray. Amen.

7

Everlasting Father, please help me to study the bible (which is your word) always. Enable me with grace to stay consistent with your word so that I can gain knowledge and wisdom needed to live a successful life on earth, and also to be counted worthy to enter your eternal kingdom. For in the name of Jesus Christ I pray. Amen.

8

Father, I want to be wise and I want to obey your commandments; therefore, I ask that you please give me an ability to daily study your word. Help me to appropriately apply your word to every area of my life, so that I can have all round success. For in the name of Jesus Christ I pray. Amen.

9

O Good Lord, please enable me to daily study your word. Empower me to comply with your instructions so that I can prosper and enjoy your goodness in the land of the living. For in the name of Jesus Christ I pray. Amen.

10

Heavenly Father, I want you to be proud of me as a diligent Christian. Please help me to do my due diligence by faithfully serving you, and by consistently studying scriptures. Also, help me to maintain a stable relationship with you through prayers. For in the name of Jesus Christ I pray. Amen.

11

Eternal Rock of Ages, I am confident that you are the almighty and most powerful being. I declare my trust in you, and I know that you will meet all my expectations. You will bless me and also give me victory over all my challenges; therefore, I am determined to love and serve you forever! Please give me the grace to remain faithful to my commitment, and let me always find pleasure in serving you. For in the name of Jesus Christ I pray. Amen.

12

Almighty Father, please enable me with grace to live in the truth of your word always. Do not let me get carried away with teachings that lack bible justifications. Give me wisdom to differentiate between deceptive teachings and the true gospel. Give me strength to walk uprightly with you always, so that I can qualify for your heavenly kingdom. For in the name of Jesus Christ I pray. Amen.

13

Jehovah, please give me grace to honor you with everything I have. Let your Holy Spirit empower me to live a pleasant life before you always, so that I can qualify for more blessings. For in the name of Jesus Christ I pray. Amen.

14

Jesus Christ, please help me to focus on serving you according to expectations. Guide me through your Holy Spirit to make decisions that will make you smile with me. Help me not to compromise my decision to faithfully serve you. Enable me with grace to honorably walk before you always, so that I can qualify for your special honor. For in the name of Jesus Christ I pray. Amen.

15

Father, please help me to live a disciplined life on earth. Keep me steadfast, and let me remain immovable and non-responsive to worldly pressures. Make me a man/woman of integrity who will remain faithfully to you unto the end, so that I can receive your tremendous blessings in heaven. For in the name of Jesus Christ I pray. Amen.

PRAYER OF ALLEGIANCE

C hristians owe allegiance to God. He is our heavenly Father, and he has every right to claim complete ownership of our lives. We are required to give Him unbiased and unconditional commitment.

"And Ruth said, Intreat me not to leave thee, or to return from following after thee: for whither thou goest, I will go; and where thou lodgest, I will lodge: thy people shall be my people, and thy God my God: Where thou diest, will I die, and there will I be buried: the LORD do so to me, and more also, if ought but death part thee and me" (Ruth 1:16-17 KJV)

---

* * *

Pray the Prayer of Allegiance

Lord Jesus Christ I realized that you have suffered and died to save me, and to give me eternal life. What a wonderful and loving friend you are! I love you too. I have made up my mind to faithfully serve you from today. I confess that you are the Son of God; you are my Lord, my Savior, and my King. I will faithfully follow and serve you for the rest of my life. I give you my heartfelt praises, and I say thank you for saving my soul! Amen.

2

Dear Lord Jesus, I appreciate the fact that you came to the world to save a poor soul like me. I understand that I can only become a child of God and have a personal relationship with him through you. Therefore, I confess you Jesus Christ as my personal Lord and Savior. I confess my sins and forsake them. From now on, I will serve you with all my might, and I will serve you throughout the days of my life. Please help me to keep my promises unto the end, so that I can be acceptable to your kingdom. For in the name of Jesus Christ I pray. Amen.

3

Vanity upon vanity, the world is vanity! I am determined to follow Jesus Christ and not allow any situation to distract me from him. I have made up my mind to keep my testimony as a child of God. I stand by my word, and I will hold firm my confession of Jesus Christ to the end. Yes, Jesus Christ is the true and only Son of God sent to rescue the lost sinners. Since I believe in Jesus, my sins are forgiven and I am qualified for rapture! Jesus Christ is my personal Lord and Savior, and the devil cannot do anything to stop it. My faith is reserved in the Son of God forever! Amen.

PRAYER OF REPENTANCE

Repentance unlocks God's door of forgiveness for sinners. Everyone needs repentance to obtain God's mercy, as the scripture stated, *"For all have sinned and fall short of the glory of God"* (Romans 3:23 NIV). We must come humbly before God to ask for mercy, forgiveness, and salvation of the Lord Jesus Christ.

"If we confess our sins, he is faithful and just to forgive us our sins, and to cleanse us from all unrighteousness." (1 John 1:9 KJV)

---

* * *

Pray the Prayer of Repentance

1

Dear Jesus Christ, I understand that it is very important that I declare my faith in you; I must believe that you died for my sins and resurrected to give me life. Therefore, I affirmatively declare that I believe you died and resurrected for my sins; I confess you as my personal Lord and Savior. From now on, I will serve you with a clean and clear mind, and I will also share your resurrection story with other people so that they can believe and be saved also. Please give me the grace to remain faithful to you throughout the days of my life. For in the name of Jesus Christ I pray. Amen.

2

Dear heavenly Father, I trust you as the only living God who will live eternally. I understand that I cannot be in harmony with you until I have confessed my faith in your Son Jesus Christ. Therefore, I confess my faith in him today. I believe that Jesus is your true and only Son sent to save the world. I confess my sins and repent from them. I declare Jesus Christ as the Lord of my life, and I promise to devote my total life to him from today. Since I have confessed my faith in Jesus, I strongly believe that I am now your child - and I am heavenly bound! Praise be to your holy name for making me heavenly worthy. Praise be to you today, and praises be to your forever! Amen.

3

Savior, I have decided to faithfully serve you. I repent of my sins, and I am completely turning my back against sinful habits. Henceforth, I will make you happy by living acceptable life before you. Please give me the grace to keep my promises, and let me receive your benefits. For in the name of Jesus Christ I pray. Amen.

4

Dear Jesus Christ, I am aware that you will appear any moment from now to rapture the saints to heaven, and I want to be raptured also.

Therefore, I repent of my sins and I confess you Jesus Christ at my Lord and Savior. I will faithfully serve you from now on; please write my name in the book of life and let me remain rapture-able to heaven. For in the name of Jesus Christ I pray. Amen.

5

Dear God, I understand that Christianity is a religion that was founded based on the fact that Jesus Christ is the only savior that leads people to your kingdom. I understand that all I need to become saved is to confess Jesus Christ as Lord and accept him as my personal Savior; therefore, I confess him (Jesus Christ) as the Son of God, and I accept him as my personal savior. I also confess my sins and repent from them. From now on, I will obey your command-ments, and I will faithfully serve you throughout the days of my life. Please give me the grace to keep my commitment until I see you in heaven to enjoy your everlasting peace. For in the name of Jesus Christ I pray. Amen.

6

Savior, I do not want to lose your treasured gift of eternal life; there-fore, I am sorry for all my sins, and I repent of them all. I will make things right from today on. Please equip me with your Holy Spirit to always meet your expectations, and keep me fit for your kingdom. For in the name of Jesus Christ I pray. Amen.

7

Father, I know that you love sinners but you hate their sins; therefore, I am determined to forsake my sins and come to you. I am sorry for all my past mistakes, and I repent of them. From now on, I will serve you with all my heart and all my strength. I will do my best to obey your instructions and please you. Please write my name in the book of life, and count me worthy to partake in your kingdom. For in the name of Jesus Christ I pray. Amen.

8

Almighty God, I am sorry if I have failed to honor my promises to you. I repent today, and I am determined to mend my broken relationship with you. I redeem all my pledges, and I will make you happy with my offerings. In fact, I will bring a special thanksgiving offering to you, and I will share the testimony of your goodness in my life to all people. Please grant me the grace to fulfill all my promises, and let me remain your favorite child. For in the name of Jesus Christ I pray. Amen.

9

I have learned that it is dangerous to engage in any action that can provoke your anger. Therefore, I am determined to operate within the scope of your mercy. I am sorry for all my past wrong deeds, and I ask you to please forgive me. From now on, I will serve you with the integrity of my heart. I believe in your Son Jesus Christ, and I accept him as my personal Lord and Savior. Please write my name in the book of life, and let it be well with me throughout the days of my life. For in the name of Jesus Christ I pray. Amen.

10

I confess that you are the living Son of God who has died for my sins. You died on the cross and resurrected from the grave to give me eternal life. I believe you, and I accept you as my personal Lord and Savior. As from today, I declare myself a "Born-Again Christian." I will follow and serve you for the rest of my life. Amen.

11

Dear God, I praise you for saving me through your beloved Son Jesus Christ. I understand that you have not saved me as a result of my personal works, but you have saved me through grace. Therefore, my life will remain dedicated to the praise of your name! I will praise you always for saving me through grace. Please, I ask for more grace to remain faithful to you. Do not let me abuse my salvation with sin, but help me to live a sanctified life that will remain fit for your kingdom. Empower me through your Holy Spirit to keep focus and remain serving you until the end of my life, so that I can meet you in heaven. For in the name of Jesus Christ I pray. Amen.

12

Dear Jesus Christ, I believe that you are God in human form. Since I have known you as the Son of God, I would also be confident to call you God. Meanwhile, I understand that the requirement set for people to go to heaven is that they must believe that you are the Son of God, and they must confess you as Lord (John 3:16; Romans 10:9). Therefore, I have chosen to meet all requirements. I confess you Jesus Christ as the Son of God (God in human flesh) and accept you as my personal Lord and Savior. Amen.

13

Dear Jesus Christ, I do not want to go to hell fire, but I want to go to heaven. Therefore, I confess that you are the Son of God who has died for the sin of the whole world. I accept you Jesus Christ as my personal Lord and Savior; I repent of my sins, and I will faithfully serve you from now on, and throughout the days of my life. So help me God! Amen.

14

Dear Jesus Christ, I believe that you are the bread of life that comes from God, and I confess you as my personal Lord and Savior. Hence-forth, I will serve you with all my might, and I will follow you unto the end. For in the name of Jesus Christ I pray. Amen.

15

I am sorry for all my sins, and I repent of them all. I give you my life today, and I confess my faith in your Son Jesus Christ that he is Lord. I believe that Jesus died and resurrected to give me eternal life; I confess my faith in him, and I accept him as my personal Lord and Savior. I promise to faithfully serve Jesus Christ throughout the days of my life. Amen.

16

Dear Jesus Christ, I believe that you are the Messiah the Savior of the world. You are the Son of God sent to save the world. I believe you with all my heart and I commit everything I have to you today. I give you my complete life, and I accept you as my personal Lord and Savior. I believe that I am now a born again Christian, and heaven is my final destination! Please uphold me to faithfully serve you unto the end. For in the name of Jesus Christ I pray. Amen.

17

Savior, I understand that I cannot lose any good thing for being your child, but I can only gain. Therefore, I am determined to be your child today! I confess your Son Jesus Christ as my Lord, and I accept him as my personal Savior. I confess my sins and I forsake them. Please release your unconquerable Spirit upon me. Let him empower me to be an overcomer! Let him energize me to start living a triumphant life from today. Let your Holy Spirit empower me to triumph throughout the days of my life. For in the name of Jesus Christ I pray. Amen.

18

Dear God, I want to go to heaven therefore; I am determined to become a born-again Christian. I confess your Son Jesus Christ as my personal Lord and Savior. I believe he died for my sins and resurrected. I also believe that I can only receive forgiveness of sins through him. Therefore, I confess my sins and repent from them. I declare my total life for Jesus Christ as from today. I will serve him today, and throughout the days of my life. Amen.

19

Dear Jesus Christ, I believe in your death and resurrection. I also believe in the Holy Communion that you started to register believers' covenant and commitment to your death and resurrection. Therefore, please help me to remain fit to participate in the Holy Communion; let it result in a renewal of my commitment to serving you throughout the days of my life. Let me remain rapturable so that I can partake in your Holy Communion in heaven also. For I have faithfully asked God to meet all these expectations in your name - Jesus Christ. Amen.

20

Dear Jesus Christ, I believe that you are the Son of God who died for sinners. You died on the cross for my sins and resurrected on the third day to give me the gift of eternal life. Therefore, I believe that you are the savior. I confess you as my Lord, and I accept you as my personal Savior. I confess my sins and I forsake them. I ask for your grace to remain faithful to you, and I will serve you throughout the days of my life. Please write my name in the book of life. For in the name of Jesus Christ I pray. Amen.

21

Father, I understand that sin can create a barrier between you and me; therefore, I am determined to run from sin. I ask for your grace to live a holy and acceptable life before you so that I can qualify for your blessings. Please bless me on earth, and also count me worthy to receive your heavenly blessings. Please let your grace be sufficient for me so that I can live a satisfying life before you always. For in the name of Jesus Christ I pray. Amen.

22

Dear God, please forgive me of any wicked act that I have involved myself. I am sorry for every evil act that I have committed. I repent from all my wickedness today, and I will never return to them again! I am now determined to do things rightly. I will exercise adequate and impartial judgments; I will not exploit anyone for my selfish gain; I will treat people under my watch fairly and equally. I will be contented with whatever I have, and I will not be envious of others. Help me to be honest in dealing with you and other people, so that it can be well with me throughout the days of my life. For in the name of Jesus Christ I pray. Amen.

23

Ancient of Days, I ask you to please forgive all my sins. Please enable me with grace to serve you with godly fear. Help me to maintain a consistent relationship with you, and help me to serve you with purity. Empower me through your Spirit to make conscious efforts to satisfy you at all time, so that it can be well with me throughout the days of my life. For in the name of Jesus Christ I pray. Amen.

24

My loving God, I admit that I am a sinner! I am sorry for everything that I have done wrong. Today, I repent of those sins, and I ask for your forgiveness. Please fill me with your Holy Spirit to always obey your instructions. Empower me to do things that are acceptable in your sight. Let the relationship that exists between us remain strong, and let me remain your true child. Keep me worthy to receive your blessings in this life and in heaven also. Please let me remain reputable always. For in the name of Jesus Christ I pray. Amen.

25

I yield my complete life to Jesus Christ today, and I accept him as my personal Lord and Savior! Since Jesus is the only way that leads to heaven, I will remain steadfast with him. No more sin and no more relationship with the devil. Henceforth, my life belongs to God and I will serve him forever! Amen.

PRAYER OF INTERCESSION

Intercession or intercessory prayer is offered to God as believers stand in gap for other people. As Christians, we must not be obsessed with our needs only, but we must intercede for others and ask God to meet their needs also. The Bible says:

"Again I say unto you, that if two of you shall agree on earth as touching anything that they shall ask, it shall be done for them of my Father which is in heaven. For where two or three are gathered together in my name, there am I in the midst of them."(Matthew 18:19- 20 KJV)

---

* * *

Pray the Prayer of Intercession

Dear Jesus Christ, I ask you to please make me an instrument of restoration to backsliding Christians. Energize me to pray, care, and proactively engage them until they are fully restored into your love. At the same time, I am using this opportunity to pray for every Christian who has lost his/her first love, to be restored. I ask the Almighty God to restore them into true and effective worship. I pray that Christ rekindles his fire in them so that they can continue to serve God in Spirit and truth. May the Holy Spirit possess my brothers and sisters that are turning back from the true love of God! May the power of God rest on all the saints to remain steadfast until the day of Christ appearance on earth. May faithful brothers and sisters remain focus to the end so that we can all shout "Hosanna" and sing songs of victory. For in the name of Jesus Christ I pray. Amen.

2

Dear God, please help me to be sensitive not to give your due glory to a mortal man or woman. Let me offer you due glory and honor at all times. In addition, give me the grace to respect your servants so that I can incur your blessings. Help me to pray and offer necessary assistance for your servants, so that they can be motivated to serve you more. Please bless me also as I endeavor to obey all your instructions. For in the name of Jesus Christ I pray. Amen.

3

Dear Jesus Christ, please save people throughout the world. Touch their hearts to realize that you have died for their sins. Let them respond to you and be saved. Let all people – irrespective of their religion, ethnicity and culture – accept you as the Son of God. Let them confess you as their personal Lord and Savior, so that they can be accepted into heaven. Also, I ask you to please empower your servants throughout the world to preach your undiluted gospel that would convert sinners into genuine repentance. For in the name of Jesus Christ I pray. Amen.

4

Dear Lord Jesus Christ, please redeem our churches again. Please make your blood shed on the cross become relevant again in our churches again! Let our church leaders start to fear and obey your instructions; let the church members take their heavenly mandates seriously. Let the truth of your gospel be preached from our church altars; let true love be demonstrated among brethren. Please, establish the standard of your righteousness in our churches so that people of this generation can have good a legacy to pass down to the coming ones. When the clock finally stop working and the world comes to an end, please make our churches receive a royal welcome in heaven as a body of saints adored for her husband. Please do this and much more! For in the name of Jesus Christ I pray. Amen.

5

Dear heavenly God, you are the first and the last; you are the final authority, and no one can question you. My life goal is to be humble before you and give you due honor. Please give me the grace to do so. Empower me to arrogate every victory I have to the praise of your name. I also pray that you will enlighten people to realize the greatness of your power over their situations so that they can praise you. For in the name of Jesus Christ I pray. Amen.

PRAYER TO HONOR GOD'S SERVANTS

I t is God's desire that believers honor one another. We must specially honor those that minister in his vineyard. Paul told the Thessalonians,

---

"Now we ask you, brothers, to respect those who work hard among you, and are over you in the Lord and who admonish you. Hold them in the highest regard in love because of their work. Live in peace with each other" (*1 Thessalonians 5:12-13 KJV*))

---

* * *

Pray for Grace to Honor God's Servants

1

Father, please teach me how to honor you and respect your servants.

Do not let me disrespect you and your servants, so that I would not be punished. Enable me to treat your servants well and respect them so that I can receive your blessings. Please let me fear you, and let me obey all your commandments so that I can prosper in the land of the living. For in the name of Jesus Christ I pray. Amen.

2

Dear God, please enable me with grace to give you due honor at all times. Do not let me disrespect you, but let me serve you with dignity and honor. Let your supernatural power bring me blessing, and let it be well with me throughout the days of my life. For in the name of Jesus Christ I pray. Amen.

3

Almighty God, I understand that you will bless me if I respect your servants, and you will punish me if I disrespect them. Therefore, I pray that you please help me to be cautious of my attitudes towards your servants. Let me respect and care for them; let me minister to their needs. Also, give me the grace to remember your servants in my prayers. Please bless me as I remember to minister to people that represent you on earth. For in the name of Jesus Christ I pray. Amen.

4

Father God, please help me to honor you and respect your servants so that I can have my expected blessings. Do not let me underestimate your servants, and do not let me despise their messages. Enable me to trust the leadership of your Holy Spirit so that I can prosper throughout the days of my life. For in the name of Jesus Christ I pray. Amen.

5

Jehovah, I want you to give me the ability to mind my own business. Do not let me meddle with your business uninvited. Help me to be sensitive enough to understand whatever activity I should be involved and what I should not. Please enable me to obey all your commandments, so that I can receive positive rewards on earth and in heaven. For in the name of Jesus Christ I pray. Amen.

6

Holy Spirit, I understand that gospel ministers are your ambassadors on earth; therefore, give me the grace to honor them. Empower me to do whatever thing I have in capacity to minister to their needs, and let me be a source of courage to their families. I also pray that you give all your servants peace and joy so that they can continue to do your good works for humanity, and for your kingdom. For in the name of Jesus Christ I pray. Amen.

PRAYER OF OBEDIENCE TO GOD

Obedience to God is a proof of our love for Him. It demonstrates our commitment and faithfulness to God. Obedience opens God's door of blessings to our lives. The Bible says:

"But be ye doers of the word, and not hearers only, deceiving your own selves." (James 1:22 KJV)

* * *

Pray for a Heart of Obedience

1

Dear God, please give me a humble heart to yield to your instructions at all times, so that I can prosper. Help me to obey you and let me be flexible for Holy Spirit's guidance. Let me follow when you lead, and let me be willing to receive your blessings whenever you are ready to hand them over. For in the name of Jesus Christ I pray. Amen.

2

Father, I realized that you will perform great wonders for anyone who faithfully serve and obey your instructions. Therefore, I want to obey you and maintain good a relationship with you. Please help me to shun every form of ungodliness so that I can enjoy you deeply. Let me love and serve you well, and let me qualify to receive your undaunted blessings on earth and in heaven. For in the name of Jesus Christ I pray. Amen.

3

Jehovah, please do not let me provoke you to receive punishments. Let me carefully obey your commandments so that I can prosper in the land of the living. For in the name of Jesus Christ I pray. Amen.

4

Dear heavenly Father, please make me an obedient child. Let me listen and obey your instructions. Give me the ability to do whatever you ask me to do. Do not let me provoke your judgment with disobedience. Enable me to always be conscious that "you see all things and you will appropriately judge all things – either with blessings or disciplines." For in the name of Jesus Christ I pray. Amen.

PRAYER FOR GODLY DECISIONS

Jesus warned Believers not to judge others, lest we be judged ourselves. Jesus also charged his disciples not to judge according to flesh but have Godly judgment – Which is praise-worthy. It was affirmed in the scripture:

"For with what judgment ye judge, ye shall be judged: and with what measure ye mete, it shall be measured to you again. And why beholdest thou the mote that is in thy brother's eye, but considerest not the beam that is in thine own eye? Or how wilt thou say to thy brother, Let me pull out the mote out of thine eye; and, behold, a beam is in thine own eye? Thou hypocrite, first cast out the beam out of thine own eye; and then shalt thou see clearly to cast out the mote out of thy brother's eye. Give not that which is holy unto the dogs, neither cast ye your pearls before swine, lest they trample them under their feet, and turn again and rend you".(Matthew 7:1-5 KJV)

* * *

Pray to Exercise Godly Judgment

1

Dear God, please help me to treat other people fairly and equally. Do not let me give preferential treatment to anyone, but help me to treat everyone with respect and love. Let me apply godly fear to whatever I do so that I can receive your blessings and not curses. Let me be a channel of blessing to all people so that your name can be praised at all times. For in the name of Jesus Christ I pray. Amen.

2

Dear God, please guide my steps not to seek counsels from ungodly people. Assist me to seek godly counselors who may guide me into making the right decisions. Help me to prayerfully consider any counsel before I take an action. Do not let me rush into judgment and regret afterward. Rather, let your Holy Spirit counsel, comfort, and empower me to appropriately make decisions that will result in positive benefits. For in the name of Jesus Christ I make my requests. Amen.

3

Dear God, please teach me how to follow your instructions so that I can have an expected victory over my life situations. Let me follow your instruction whenever you lead so that I can prosper! Let victory be my portion today, tomorrow, and everyday of my life. For in the name of Jesus Christ I pray. Amen.

PRAYER OF UNITY IN CHRISTENDOM

U nity to God is more important than diversity that many in today's world are celebrating. Christians must stay together as the scripture says,

---

"Finally, be ye all of one mind, having compassion one of another, love as brethren, be pitiful, be courteous". (1 Peter 3:8 KJV)

---

* * *

Pray for Unity in Christendom

1

Holy Spirit, please enable the church to serve you with openness and love. Let brethren operate in love, and let us submit to the leadership of your Holy Spirit. Also, mortify every work of flesh in our lives, so that we can faithfully serve you and be truthfully committed to one another. For in the name of Jesus Christ I pray. Amen.

2

Father, please bring the body of Christ together and let us act as a theme. Grant each believer a loving heart to accommodate his/her fellow Christians. Let every denomination put prejudice aside and submit to your will by demonstrating true love toward others. Enable the fold of Christ to raise the banner of love to uphold your righteousness in every community. Please help the church to overcome all its challenges, so that your name can be praised throughout the world. For in the name of Jesus Christ I pray. Amen.

3

Jehovah, please help the church to stay together to achieve its heavenly mandate. Help brethren to worship you together in spirit and in truth. Also, help brethren to minister to the needs of each other in love. Let every brother and sister in Christ make personal efforts that are necessary to keep the body of Christ together in unity. At end of this world, let brethren converge at your feet in paradise to enjoy endless fellowship with you. For in the name of Jesus Christ I pray. Amen.

4

Father, please give me the grace to love other people genuinely. Let me have a positive interest of other people in mind. Help me to demonstrate selfless love towards my fellow believers, and let me make positive contributions to their lives. Please let me receive benefits of true love in this life, and the one to come! For in the name of Jesus Christ I pray. Amen.

5

Ancient of Days, please save the Christian community from bitterness and rage of division that hinders our operations. Let brethren respectfully deal with each other. Enable us to find common ground that would offer us platform to preach your unbiased gospel. Help us to lay aside our differences, and let us respect bible teachings. Let your Holy Spirit give us proper interpretations of your word, and let us adequately apply them into our lives. Help the church to be sensitive and corporately launch crusades that will uphold your righteous standard and lead people to receive your salvation. Let us be your true ambassadors on earth so that we can receive your eternal rewards in heaven. For in the name of Jesus Christ I pray. Amen.

6

Dear Jesus Christ, please enable believers to operate in love. Let us love and care for each other genuinely. Let brethren minister to each other in prayers and encouragements. Let brethren provide for each other in food, clothes, money, and other necessities. Enable us to visit our fellows in the hospital; let us offer moral supports for people in need. Let your genuine love be real in Christian fold so that your glory can radiate in our lives with signs and wonders. For in the name of Jesus Christ I pray. Amen.

7

Dear God, please keep brethren together in unity. Encourage us to put our differences aside so that we can effectively praise you with one mind. Release your overflowing grace and anointing on all brethren as we make significant efforts to promote your name in love. For in the name of Jesus Christ I pray. Amen.

8

Jehovah, please bind the Christian body together in unity. Let both the church leaders and their members submit to you. Let denominations subject their private doctrines for bible standards; let all churches and brethren join their hands together to promote your righteousness in our lands. Let the church prioritize gospel evangelization, and let them intensely engage in it so that unbelievers throughout the world can have an opportunity to be saved. Please do not let brethren fail you anymore, but let us actively and faithfully serve you so that we can be blessed on earth and in heaven. For in the name of Jesus Christ I pray. Amen.

PRAYER OF REVIVAL FOR THE CHURCH

To "revive" means to "live again." It is important that the church continue to pray for revival, so as to be effective instrument in the hands of God for expanding his kingdom. The Bible says:

"Wilt thou not revive us again: that thy people may rejoice in thee. " (Psalms 85:6: KJV)

* * *

Pray for Church Revival

1

O Lord, please wake up the church from its deep sleep! The church has become cold, and brethren have lost their drive to spiritually seek your help for a solution over their problems. Please revive our local churches and denominations again! Enable us to seek your face for guidance and instructions. Let brethren prioritize prayer and holiness to other influences. Let brethren cooperate with you, so that we can experience signs and wonders like the early days church. Uphold our leaders, and rescue them from carnality and selfish interests. Let the church leaders and members prosper on earth, and also fit for your rapture. For in the name of Jesus Christ I pray. Amen.

2

In the name of Jesus Christ, I pray for fellow Christians and myself that God give us the spirit of love. May the Almighty God empower us to love each other! May the churches put segregation aside to love and serve God with the spirit of unity! May pride, stubbornness, and self-righteous spirits be subdued in Christian fold! May all children of God feel and experience genuine love of God that is beyond human comprehension! May it be well for all believers in Christ today, tomorrow, and forevermore! Amen.

3

Father, Let both the church leaders and their members submit to you. Let denominations subject their private doctrines for bible standards; let all churches and brethren join their hands together to promote your righteousness in our lands. Let the church prioritize gospel evangelization, and let them intensely engage in it so that unbelievers throughout the world can have an opportunity to be saved. Please do not let brethren fail you anymore, but let us actively and faithfully serve you so that we can be blessed on earth and in heaven. For in the name of Jesus Christ I make all these requests.

Amen.

PRAYER OF VICTORY

The word victory must remain a firm and sure term for everyone who believes in God. Christians are to utilize the authority in the name of Jesus Christ to prevail over the power of darkness. Believers must always rejoice since we have provision of victory in Jesus Christ. It is written:

"Nay, in all these things we are more than conquerors through him that loved us". (Romans 8:37 KJV)

---

* * *

Pray the Prayers of Victory

1

Father, please give me the grace to be steadfast in faith. Let your Holy Spirit empower me to stay upright to overcome trials and temptations. Let me sing songs of victory, and let your testimony never depart from my life. At the end of my earthly journey, let me hear your heavenly voice "Welcome my good servant." For in the name of Jesus Christ I pray. Amen.

2

Almighty Father, please do all that it takes to defend me against my adversaries. Fight my battles and earn me your victory. Please earn me your grace and mercy, and let my expectations be fulfilled upon my enemies. For in the name of Jesus Christ I pray. Amen.

3

I am not an ordinary person; I enjoy the immunity of God. Since I am a son/daughter of the Almighty God, no force on earth can harm me. I understand this fact, and I am assured that his security radar will ever watch over me. Jehovah will defeat Satan's works in my life, and help me achieve victory. For in the name of Jesus Christ I have made my declarations. Amen!

PRAYER OF PROTECTION

E veryone wants protection and freedom – Christians are not exempted. Believers must live to enjoy God's benefits and serve him with the liberty of our spirit. The Bible says:

"I have set the LORD always before me: because he is at my right hand, I shall not be moved." (Psalms 16:8 KJV)

---

* * *

Pray the Prayer of Protection

1

Father, I desire your divine protections and provisions. Therefore, I ask that you please make me your true child. Let my relationship with you be consistent, and help me to reserve my confidence in you throughout the days of my life. For in the name of Jesus Christ I pray. Amen.

2

Glory to God for he is my father and I am his son/daughter! I am secured in his loving arms. He will keep and save me from enemies' assaults. Jehovah will keep watch over me and rescue my soul from wicked people. Since I am a child of God, there shall be no mountain so high and no valley so low, God will level them all for me! I am confident that the promises of God over me are irrevocable! I am blessed in the morning and I am blessed in the evening. In fact, I am blessed throughout the days of my life. The joy of the Lord is my strength and his testimony shall remain fresh in my mouth - forever! Thanks to Jesus Christ for granting me remarkable testimonies in God. Amen.

3

Dear God, please help me to trust you in all situations, and help me to affirm trust that you will help in every situation that comes my way. Do not let me take laws into my hands against the adversaries. I know that you can help, and you will surely help me! Therefore, grant me patience and grace to allow your full operations in my life. Let me allow you to handle every matter in a way that will honor and glorify your holy name, and bless my life. For in the name of Jesus Christ your Son I pray. Amen.

4

Dear Jesus Christ, what a wonderful savior you are! You never sleep or slumber, but you are keeping constant watch over me. I love you so much! Since you are my confidant and security, I will follow you throughout the days of my life. I yield my complete life to you from now and forever more! I will also tell the whole world that you are the Savior of the world, and all people should follow you! Amen.

PRAYER OF HUMILITY

Humility is a direct opposite of pride. Christians are expected to be humble like Jesus Christ "Who, being in very nature God, did not consider equality with God something to be used to his own advantage" (Philippians 2:6).

"For whosoever exalteth himself shall be abased; and he that humbleth himself shall be exalted." (Luke 14:11 KJV)

---

* * *

Pray the Prayer of Humility

1

Ancient of Days, please make me a humble person. Give me the grace to demonstrate sincere humility like your Son Jesus Christ who submitted himself to ridicule and dishonor for the purpose of saving humanity. Help me to submit myself to you also; let me think about you more and serve you better. To demonstrate my sincerity, I therefore, submit on my knees today and confess my sins and declare Jesus Christ as my Lord. I declare that he (Jesus) is Lord, and I accept him as my personal Savior. From now on, I will serve Jesus with all my strength, and I will do this for the rest of my life! For in the name of Jesus Christ I pray. Amen.

2

Dear Lord, if you can use anyone, use me! I will consider it an honor to serve you with all my strength. If you choose me, I will run fast, and I will loudly proclaim your goodness throughout the earth. I will serve you in the morning, afternoon, and evening. In fact, I will infiltrate the whole world with your good news, and I will fly your banner very high. I repeat again: "Lord, if you can use anyone, use me!" in Jesus Name I pray. Amen.

3

Dear God, please do not let me abuse your grace in my life. Help me to fear and carefully follow all your instructions so that I can prosper in life and ministry. I also pray that you frustrate all enemies' schemes aimed to sabotage your grace in my life. Let my enemies fail; let me serve you well, and let me receive your goodly rewards in this life – and in heaven also. For in the name of Jesus Christ I make my requests. Amen.

PRAYER OF ABTAINENCE FROM WICKEDNESS

J esus made us to understand that the end time is like the day of Noah. God will judge our present earth as He did to Noah's generation. The Bible warned us against every form of wickedness:

"Despise not prophesying. Prove all things; hold fast that which is good. Abstain from all appearance of evil. And the very God of peace sanctify you wholly; and I pray God] your whole spirit and soul and body be preserved blameless unto the coming of our Lord Jesus Christ. Faithful is he that calleth you, who also will do it". (I Thessalonians 5:20-24 KJV)

---

* * *

Pray for Abstinence from Wickedness

1

Father, please count me out of wicked people. I do not want to be categorized with evil people! Help me to love and fear you always. Enable be to love other people as well. Please bless me today, tomorrow, and for the rest of my life. For in the name of Jesus Christ I pray. Amen.

2

Dear God, please help me to respond to hateful situations with godly attitude! When circumstances are rough and rash, help me to respond positively so that devil can be ashamed, and your name can be glorified. Please empower me through Holy Spirit to remain your good child unto the end of my life, so that I can be qualified to rejoice with you in heaven. For in the name of Jesus Christ I make my requests. Amen.

3

Father, please save the Christian community from bitterness and rage of division that hinders our operations. Let brethren respectfully deal with each other. Enable us to find common ground that would offer us platform to preach your unbiased gospel. Help us to lay aside our differences, and let us respect bible teachings. Let your Holy Spirit give us proper interpretations of your word, and let us adequately apply them into our lives. Help the church to be sensitive and corporately launch crusades that will uphold your righteous standard and lead people to receive your salvation. Let us be your true ambassadors on earth so that we can receive your eternal rewards in heaven. For in the name of Jesus Christ I make my requests. Amen.

PRAYER TO ENDURE PERSECUTION

We live in time and age when systematic persecution of saints is at the horizon. Christians suffer hostility and direct attacks for our belief. The Bible encourages us to remain steadfast in God.

"But I say unto you, Love your enemies, bless them that curse you, do good to them that hate you, and pray for them which despitefully use you, and persecute you" (Matthew 5:44 KJV)

---

* * *

Pray for Grace to Endure Persecution

1

Help me to remain strong during persecution, and let me keep my faith unto the end. Please anoint me with oil of gladness to continue sharing your gospel throughout the word. For in the name of Jesus Christ I pray. Amen.

2

Dear God, please help me to respond to hateful situations with godly attitude! When circumstances are rough and rash, help me to respond positively so that devil can be ashamed, and your name can be glorified. Please empower me through Holy Spirit to remain your good child unto the end of my life, so that I can be qualified to rejoice with you in heaven. For in the name of Jesus Christ I make my requests. Amen.

3

Dear God, if I do not trust you who else should I trust? No one! My goal is to trust you under whatever condition. Therefore, I pray that you please endow me with grace to trust you. Empower me through your Holy Spirit to confide and invite you into the situations of my life, so that I can prosper. Please bless me and let me enjoy your goodness throughout the days of my life. For in the name of Jesus Christ I make my requests. Amen.

4

In the name of Jesus Christ, I command the challenges of my life to bow! I rebuke Satan and I command him to remove his dirty hands from my life. I command sickness, poverty, failure, sin and all works of Satan to cease in my life. I obtain my victory today, tomorrow, and forever in the name of Jesus Christ. Amen!

PRAYER OF FAITHFULNESS

People who wait on God will not be put to shame under whatever condition. They will also be confident of their future, and they will have enough courage to do God's will. The psalmist explained this well when he stated:

"Trust in the LORD, and do good; so shalt thou dwell in the land, and verily thou shalt be fed. Delight thyself also in the LORD; and he shall give thee the desires of thine heart. Commit thy way unto the LORD; trust also in him; and he shall bring it to pass. And he shall bring forth thy righteousness as the light, and thy judgment as the noonday. Rest in the LORD, and wait patiently for him: fret not thyself because of him who prosperity in his way, because of the man who bringeth wicked devices to pass. Cease from anger, and forsake wrath: fret not thyself in any wise to do evil. For evildoers shall be cut off: but those that wait upon the LORD, they shall inherit the earth." (Psalm 37:3-9 KJV)

---

* * *

Pray the Prayers of Faithfulness

1

Jehovah, please help me to faithfully serve you and care for other people. Do not let me practice eye-service, but let me be truthful in my endeavors. Let me act as your true representative on earth, so that I can be duly rewarded in heaven. For in the name of Jesus Christ I pray. Amen.

2

Dear Lord, how best can I serve you, and how can I offer an acceptable sacrifice to you? I have realized that you cannot be deceived with a dishonored gift – no matter how significant it appears! Please help me to serve you without ulterior motives. Let me be sincere with my gifts, and let them come from a pure heart. Let my sacrifices of thanksgiving satisfy you, and enable me to maintain consistent services to you, so that I can be qualified to receive your blessings. For in the name of Jesus Christ I pray. Amen.

3

Father, please do not let me make empty promises to you, but help me to honor you with my promises. Please forgive me of all unre-deemed vows. I repent today, and I will immediately redeem all the pledges that I have made to you in the past. After I redeem my pledges, let my delayed blessings be released. Henceforth, let me satisfy you with pleasant offerings, and let my gifts gladdens your heart towards me – so that I can prosper in the land of the living. For in the name of Jesus Christ I pray. Amen.

4

Father, please keep me steadfast with you at all time, and help me to relate to you as a friend and a father. Enable me to share my thoughts with you and also seek your directions. Give me the grace to follow your instructions and not yield to the desires of the flesh. Empower me through your Holy Spirit to relate with you with integrity. Let me serve you with dignity and honor, and let all my services be acceptable in your sight. Please count me among people that will receive your imperishable rewards in heaven. For in the name of Jesus Christ I pray. Amen.

5

Jehovah, I believe that Jesus Christ is your only Son sent to save the world. Through him, I receive salvation and gift of eternal life, since there is no any other name under heaven through which anyone can be saved. I swear my allegiance to Jesus Christ, and I am determined to serve him throughout the days of my life - so help me God! Amen.

6

Almighty, I realize that you want my perfect attention, and you want me to maintain a consistent relationship with you; therefore, I ask for your grace to remain faithful and meet your holiness expectations. Energize me through your Holy Spirit to walk in your ways so that I can prosper throughout the days of my life. For in the name of Jesus Christ I pray. Amen.

7

Loving father, I understand that I am a child of light and I must not associate with children of darkness. Therefore, I ask you to help me maintain a disciplined attitude and not make friendship with worldly people. Help me to comply with your godly standard that will keep me qualified for your blessings. For in the name of Jesus Christ I pray. Amen.

8

Dear heavenly Father, what a privilege I have to be your child! I am your choice child and I am an apple of your eyes. I believe that you will go any extent to defend your glory in my life. You will rescue me from evil, and you will give me upper hands over my adversaries. In fact, with my very eyes, I will see my expectations fulfilled on my adversaries! All that I ask is the grace to remain your true child. Please keep my feet steadfast in your presence, and let me remain fit to inherit your kingdom. For in the name of Jesus Christ I pray. Amen.

9

Dear God, please teach me how to offer my best sacrifices to you at all time. Let my offerings be pure, and let them be acceptable in your presence. Please let my efforts incur your blessings, and let me receive your riches and honor that follow acts of obedience. For in the name of Jesus Christ I pray. Amen.

10

O Lord, I ask you to please make me a faithful servant who will remain loyal to you always. I also pray for your other servants throughout the world. Please give everyone courage and strength to serve you well. Empower us to consider serving you our prime goal. Let your servants' efforts bear fruits for your kingdom; let our various efforts lead to the salvation of souls so that devil can be ashamed and your name be praised. For in the name of Jesus Christ I pray. Amen.

11

I thank you God for you are the Lord of lords and God of gods. For your goodness is far-reaching, and your wisdom is unsearchable. You are a wonderful God at all time. You are the husband of the widows; wife of the widowers, and father of the orphans. Your faithfulness reaches from coast to coast; it extends from north to south, and from east to west. I thank you, God for all your goodness in my life. Thanks again God, and I say Amen!

12

O Lord, I have been challenged to realize that my extra efforts will call for your special attentions. Therefore, I ask that you give me the grace to serve you better. Help me to make you happy by adding more efforts to my Christian services, so that I can be exceptionally blessed in this life, and in heaven also. For in the name of Jesus Christ I pray. Amen.

PRAYER OF PEACE

The only permanent peace is the one that Jesus Christ purchased for Christians with his blood. This peace will keep us going even when it seems as if the world is falling apart around us. God's peace reign over any crisis of life. The Bible says:

"Peace I leave with you; my peace I give you. I do not give to you as the world gives. Do not let your hearts be troubled and do not be afraid" (John 14:27 NIV).

Pray the Prayer of Peace

1

May the peace of God that surpasses all human understanding be upon all the saints of God. May the church prosper in all his deeds.

May God help my fellow Christians to overcome their challenges. May the Christian community live in peace and may we all have an abundance of the Holy Spirit to run successful ministries and enjoy all God's benefits. For I have made all these declarations in the name of our Lord Jesus Christ – and all the churches and brethren throughout the world say "Amen!"

2

Jehovah, please teach me how to pray to you for help during difficult situations. When I pray, please listen. Answer my prayers and grant every request of my heart. Let me live in joy, peace, and prosperity throughout the days of my life. For in the name of Jesus Christ I pray. Amen.

3

Dear God, I praise you for your guaranteed peace, protection, and provision that you have promised those who believe in you. Since I am a born again Christian, I am bound to succeed. I will enjoy your benefits of peace, joy and victory on earth. I will enjoy your benefits in heaven also. Again, I praise you for your benefits! In appreciation for your blessings, I will serve you throughout the days of my life. Please give me your grace to do so. For I pray in the name of Jesus Christ. Amen.

OVERCOMERS PRAYER

Any Christian who knows how to apply Christ's authority will live an overcomer's life. We must exercise Christ's authority to defeat Satan and live in victory.

"For whatsoever is born of God overcometh the world: and this is the victory that overcometh the world, even our faith." (1 John 5:4 KJV)

---

* * *

Pray Overcomer's Prayers

1

Almighty God, please teach me how to pray and trust you in all situations. Enable me with strength to completely trust you over every situation of my life. Please let me reap faith reward by experiencing a breakthrough in every area of my life. Let the songs of your testimony ever fill my mouth. For in the name of Jesus Christ I pray. Amen.

2

Father, I understand that you are the final authority over all things. Whatever you say or do cannot be altered, therefore, I choose to trust you. I ask for your provision and protection so that my joy can be full. Please give me the joy of your salvation so that my name can be permanently registered in the book of life. For in the name of Jesus Christ I pray. Amen.

3

Dear God, please teach me how to trust you during adversity. Help me to express my absolute trust in you during a difficult moment. Give me strength to declare a statement of faith that you are in charge of my situation. As I trust you, let my trial turn to testimony! Give me victory so that I can share the testimony of your goodness among your saints. For in the name of Jesus Christ I pray. Amen.

PRAYER OF GENUINE LOVE

J esus Christ founded the Christian faith on the principle of love. Christians are commanded to wholeheartedly love God and one another. John, one of Christ's disciples and closest friends made us to understand that anyone who abides in love abides in God, and God in him. The Bible says:

And we have known and believed the love that God hath to us. God is love; and he that dwelleth in love dwelleth in God and God in him. (1 John 4:16 KJV)

---

* * *

Pray for Genuine Love

1

Dear God, please make me a Christian that loves other people with all my heart. Help me to have a selfless attitude towards others. Let me be a part of people's solution and not their source of problems. Please let me be your true ambassador on earth, and let me serve you well. Also, let me be duly rewarded for good services whenever I come to your presence in heaven. For in the name of Jesus Christ I pray. Amen.

2

Dear Jesus Christ, please empower me to have compassion for needy people. Let me express my faith in you by loving other people. Let me be a channel of blessing to people throughout the world, so that your name can be praised. For in the name of Jesus Christ I pray. Amen.

3

Dear God, please enable me grace to demonstrate selfless love towards other people. Do not let me seek selfish gains, but help me to care with a liberal heart. I know that you will definitely bless me if I represent you well on earth, so help me to please you. Let me be your true ambassador on earth, and let me qualify to receive your heavenly rewards. For in the name of Jesus Christ I pray. Amen.

4

Lord Jesus, please help me to love other people genuinely. Let me be happy when they are happy, and let me contribute to the success of other people. Do not let me be an object of people's downfall, but their object of lifting. For in the name of Jesus Christ I pray. Amen.

5

In the name of Jesus Christ, I pray for fellow Christians and myself that God give us the spirit of love. May the Almighty God empower us to love each other! May the churches put segregation aside to love and serve God with the spirit of unity! May pride, stubbornness, and self-righteous spirits be subdued in Christian fold! May all children of God feel and experience genuine love of God that is beyond human comprehension! May it be well for all believers in Christ today, tomorrow, and forevermore! Amen.

6

Dear Jesus Christ, please empower me to have compassion for needy people. Let me express my faith in you by loving other people. Let me be a channel of blessing to people throughout the world, so that your name can be praised. For in the name of Jesus Christ I pray. Amen.

PRAYER OF RELATIONSHIP

God has always desired to have a relationship with us. Before Adam and Eve sinned in the Garden of Eden (*Genesis Chapter 3*), they knew God intimately. They related with Him personally until sin disconnected them. Christians must realize our need for God, and seek him wholeheartedly. Faith in Jesus Christ will reconnect us with God.

Behold, I stand at the door, and knock: if any man hears my voice, and open the door, I will come into him, and will sup with him, and he with me. (Revelation 3:20 KJV)

---

* * *

Pray the Prayer of Relationship

1

Father, please help me to remain focus in your presence. Help me to maintain a consistent relationship with you. Help me to find satisfaction in the habit of daily bible study and prayers. Please let your promises of prosperity be fulfilled in my life, and let me enjoy your goodness until the very end of my earthly journey. For in the name of Jesus Christ I pray. Amen.

2

Ancient of Days, my life is empty without you, and I want to have a good relationship with you. I understand that you can only relate to me if I repent from my sins; therefore, I come to you with my full confession today. I am sorry for all my sins, I confess my sins and repent from them. I request the forgiveness of my sins through your Son Jesus Christ. Please wash me clean and keep me fit to enjoy the benefits of your relationship. Please keep me fit for your kingdom also. Let it be well with me throughout the days of my life. For in the name of Jesus Christ I pray. Amen.

3

Jehovah, I do not want to fool myself by assuming that it is not necessary to have a definite relationship with you! I need you; I need your deliverance, protection, and provisions! Therefore, I am ready to give all it takes to have you in my life as my personal Lord and Savior. I yield my total life to you today; I confess your Son Jesus Christ as Lord, and I accept him as my personal Savior. From now on, I will faithfully serve you, and for the rest of my life! Thank you, God for sending your Son Jesus Christ to save my soul. For in the name of Jesus Christ I prayed. Amen.

4

Oh Lord, please help me not to form an alliance with people that care less about you. Help me to be sensitive enough to interact and form networks of people that have regards for your principles. Let me walk with people of value, so that your light may shine through me. Also, help me to be a good example for other people to emulate. Please let my services be acceptable before you always. For in the name of Jesus Christ I pray. Amen.

5

Dear Jesus Christ, please help me to be a true Christian who remains focused on you. Let me maintain a healthy relationship with you, and let me make you happy at all times. At the end of my earthly journey, let me be accepted into your kingdom to receive an imperishable crown of glory. For in the name of Jesus Christ I pray. Amen.

6

Jesus Christ, please help me to be conscious of holiness, and maintain a clean relationship with you at all times. Do not let me fall into sin, so that Satan will not take advantage of me. Help me to express genuine repentance whenever I sin against you. Let me humble myself and repent from sin so that I can receive your forgiveness. Please guide me in holiness and protect me from the enemies. Let me enjoy all your benefits throughout the days of my life. For in the name of Jesus Christ I pray. Amen.

7

Dear Jesus Christ, please do not let me serve you in vain. Do not let me waste my time by remaining a nominal Christian. Help me to maintain a serious relationship with you. Let me be your true child that complies with your holiness standards. At the end of it all, let me be welcome to heaven to receive your precious imperishable crown of glory. For in the name of Jesus Christ I pray. Amen.

PRAYER OF STRENGTH

We need divine strength because we face a stubborn enemy that constantly tempts us with sin. The strength of God is sufficient for us to overcome the enemy! The scripture stated:

"He that dwelleth in the secret place of the most High shall abide under the shadow of the Almighty. I will say of the LORD, He is my refuge and my fortress: my God; in him will I trust. Surely he shall deliver thee from the snare of the fowler, and from the noisome pestilence. He shall cover thee with his feathers, and under his wings shalt thou trust: his truth shall be thy shield and buckler. Thou shalt not be afraid for the terror by night, nor for the arrow that flieth by day; Nor for the pestilence that walketh in darkness; nor for the destruction that wasteth at noonday. A thousand shall fall at thy side, and ten thousand at thy right hand; but it shall not come nigh thee. Only with thine eyes shalt thou behold and see the reward of the wicked. Because thou hast made the LORD, which is my refuge, even the most High, thy habitation; There shall no evil *befall thee, neither shall any plague come nigh thy dwelling. For he shall give his angels charge over thee, to keep thee in all thy ways .They shall bear thee up in their hands, lest thou dash thy foot against a stone. Thou shalt tread upon the lion and adder: the young lion and the dragon shalt thou trample under feet. Because he hath set his love upon me, therefore will I deliver him: I will set him on high, because he hath known my name He shall call upon me, and I will answer him: I will be with him in trouble; I will deliver him, and honour him. With long life will I satisfy him, and shew him my salvation".(Psalm 91 vs. 1-16 KJV)*

✳ ✳ ✳

Pray the Prayer of Strength

1

Father, please give me strength to overcome Satan and live triumphantly on earth to the glorification of your holy name! Again, give me strength to remain focus and pay no damn attention to the devil and his evil agents! Let your Holy Spirit empower me to remain immovable, and to keep faithfully serving you during opposition and challenges. Also, let your Holy Spirit empower me to be watchful and prayerful so that I can keep prospering in all my ministerial activities so that light of your gospel can spread throughout the world. When my earthly race is eventually over, let me appear in your presence in heaven to hear "Well-done and welcome my servant to the joy of your Lord!" For I pray in the name of Jesus Christ. Amen.

2

Dear God, I ask you to please subdue all enemies' attacks that are wage against me. Let my enemies stumble in their evil imaginations. Give them rooms for repentance, but if they refuse, beat them down and completely incapacitate them! As for me, let me continue to fly in beautiful colors that radiate your glory. For in the name of Jesus Christ I make my requests. Amen.

3

Dear God, I believe that you are the strongest being in existence and you have power over all things. Therefore, I invite you to come to my aids and rescue me from all problems. Please confuse my enemies and let them stumble in their evil practices. Give me upper hands over my adversaries, and let me experience your divine victory. For in the name of Jesus Christ I make my requests. Amen.

PRAYER OF ABUNDANT GRACE

G race of God is without measure. We must always ask for his grace in every situation and in every area of our lives. The Bible says:

"For if by one man's offense death reigned by one; much more they which receive abundance of grace and of the gift of righteousness shall reign in life by one, Jesus Christ". (Romans 5:17 KJV)

* * *

Pray for God's Abundant Grace

1

Dear God, please do not let me abuse your grace in my life. Help me to fear and carefully follow all your instructions so that I can prosper in life and ministry. I also pray that you frustrate all enemies' schemes aim to sabotage your grace in my life. Let my enemies fail; let me serve you well, and let me receive your goodly rewards in this life – and in heaven also. For in the name of Jesus Christ I pray. Amen.

2

Ancient of Days, I understand that you require that all people must faithfully obey you and follow your instructions. Therefore, I am ready to yield my life and obey you to the fullness. I will serve and honor you as long as I live. I am utilizing this opportunity to ask for your extra grace that will enable me to satisfy you at all times. Please give me your grace so that I can prosper on earth and in heaven also. For in the name of Jesus Christ I pray. Amen.

3

Jehovah, please help me to be sensitive in the Holy Ghost at all times. Let me yield my total life unto you, and let me follow your instructions whenever you lead – so that I can enjoy your unmerited grace and favor on earth. For in the name of Jesus Christ I pray. Amen.

4

Dear God, I understand that Satan has nothing good to offer anyone; therefore, I choose to follow you. My heart desires would be to faithfully serve you and obey your instructions. I will not deviate from loving you! I will serve you with my whole heart, and I will give all it takes to make our relationship work. Please anoint me with grace and fill me with your Holy Spirit to keep my promises, and remain faithful to you unto the end. Please count me worthy of your blessings on earth and in heaven also. For in the name of Jesus Christ I pray. Amen.

PRAYER FOR UNWAVERING FAITH

T he kind of faith that can earn us God's benefits is the type that does not compromise in spite of challenges. The scripture says:

"Let us hold fast the profession of our faith without wavering; (for he is faithful that promised ;)" (Hebrew 10:23 KJV)

---

* * *

Pray the Prayer of Unwavering Faith

1

I agree that all things are possible with God; therefore, I claim my healing, blessing, and deliverance by the authority in the name of Jesus Christ. I command all situations of life to turn around to become my advantage. From now on, I claim my total victory over every life circumstances, and I declare myself a champion! For in the name of Jesus Christ I demonstrate my authority. Amen.

2

Almighty God, please give me resolute faith that will remain unshifted in the sight of any challenge. Let me be strong and hold firm to my confessions of faith in you. In fact, let Satan be ashamed because I have strong faith in you. Let me receive products of faith, which are not limited to joy, prosperity, and testimonies. For in the name of Jesus Christ I desire to have resolute faith in you. Amen!

3

Dear Lord, please help me to take Christianity seriously and apply faith to everything I do. Help me to relate with you in faith, and let me pray to you in faith. Let me demonstrate absolute confidence and believe that you will definitely grant all my requests, and you will make me live a victorious life on earth. For in the name of Jesus Christ I pray. Amen.

4

Dear Lord, I love good rewards, and I want you to give me many of them. Let me faithfully serve you so that I can qualify for your blessings. Please encourage me to stand with you at all times, even when it is no convenient! Let me be your true son/daughter/servant that would be honored on the Day of Reckoning. For in the name of Jesus Christ I pray. Amen.

5

Dear Jesus Christ, please make me strong and let me keep my faith unto the end. Give me grace and power to resist oppositions and stop their advances. Anoint me to keep the flag of your gospel flying, and let me rejoice in all ramifications of life. For in the name of Jesus Christ I pray. Amen.

6

I believe in God of miracle! I believe in the living God who is always able to deliver his children from troubles. I affirm my trust in God to earn me testimony in all areas of life. Since Jesus Christ is ever alive, I declare my victory over the enemies, and I disband their forces. I command my indefatigable victory by the authority in the name of Jesus Christ. Amen.

7

Ancient of Days, please enable me to anchor my faith in you at all times. Let me have resolute faith, and let me trust you over any challenge that comes my way. Give me victory; let me laugh, and let Satan be ashamed. For in the name of Jesus Christ I pray. Amen.

PRAYER OF VIGILANCE

C hristians are to be prayerful and watchful to live overcomer's lives on earth. We must apply the rule of the Bible to prevail over the adversaries, and enjoy God's benefits.

"Watch and pray so that you will not fall into temptation. The spirit is willing, but the flesh is weak" (Matthew 26:41 KJV)

---

* * *

Pray the Prayers of Vigilance

1

Dear Jesus Christ, please help me to be spiritually sensitive. Let me be filled with your Holy Spirit, and let me maintain a consistent attitude of praying and fasting before you so that I can always have upper hands over my adversaries. Please bless me and let me grow in grace and anointing to satisfy you at all times. For in the name of Jesus Christ I pray. Amen.

2

Dear Father, please help me to be wise and sensitive so that I will not become a victim of wicked people. Help me to abstain from people who may influence me to sin against you. Empower me to remain steadfast in faith, and let me keep my godly testimony unto the end so that I can be blessed immensely in heaven. For in the name of Jesus Christ I pray. Amen.

3

Holy Spirit, help us to be vigilant and to have the presence of mind to sense enemy's spiritual attack on us. For I Pray in Jesus Name.

ABOUT THE AUTHOR

James Taiwo is the founder and senior pastor of World Outreach Evangelical Ministry in New York City. He holds a Doctor of Theology degree and a Master of Science Degree in Environmental Engineering. A practicing civil and environmental engineer and preacher, James also plays saxophone and is an avid blogger. With the aim of diversifying the gospel to adapt to the fast-changing technology of our day, he is the publisher of Trumpet Media Ministries and author of several books, including *Bible Application Lessons and Prayers*, *The Pinnacle of Compassion*, *Who Was Jesus Really?*, *Christian Principle Guides*, and *Roadmap to Success*. James lives in New York City with his wife and children.

CONNECT WITH THE AUTHOR

Please add your honest, positive reviews of this book online. Rate this
book five stars now at
www.bit.ly/thebookofprayers

Sign up for new book alert from the author at www.bit.ly/book-alert

Visit the author's website at
www.jamestaiwo.com

Connect with the author on social media

📘 facebook.com/jamestaiwoJT

🐦 twitter.com/DrJamesTaiwoJT

🅰 amazon.com/author/jamestaiwo

ALSO BY JAMES TAIWO

Bible Application Lessons and Prayers

Bible Giants of Faith

Christian Principle Guides

Who Was Jesus, Really? - Book One

Who Was Jesus, Really? - Book Two

Who Was Jesus, Really? - Book Three

The Pinnacle of Compassion

Success Express Lane (Your Roadmap To Personal Achievement)

Made in the USA
Middletown, DE
13 August 2020